AI
Autonomous Cars
Forefront

Practical Advances in
Artificial Intelligence and Machine Learning

Dr. Lance B. Eliot, MBA, PhD

ISBN: 1-7332498-2-6
ISBN-13: 978-1-7332498-2-9

DEDICATION

To my incredible daughter, Lauren, and my incredible son, Michael.

Forest fortuna adiuvat (from the Latin; good fortune favors the brave).

CONTENTS

Acknowledgments iii

Introduction 1

Chapters

1 Eliot Framework for AI Self-Driving Cars 15

2 Essential Stats and AI Self-Driving Cars 29

3 Stats Fallacies and AI Self-Driving Cars 41

4 Driver Bullies and AI Self-Driving Cars 55

5 Sunday Drives and AI Self-Driving Cars 65

6 Face Recog Bans and AI Self-Driving Cars 75

7 States On-The-Hook and AI Self-Driving Cars 85

8 Sensors Profiting and AI Self-Driving Cars 93

9 Unruly Riders and AI Self-Driving Cars 103

10 Father's Day and AI Self-Driving Cars 113

11 Summons Feature and AI Self-Driving Cars 119

12 Libra Cryptocurrency and AI Self-Driving Cars 129

13 Systems Naming and AI Self-Driving Cars 139

14 Mid-Traffic Rendezvous and AI Self-Driving Cars 151

15 Pairing Drones and AI Self-Driving Cars 161

16 Lost Wallet Study and AI Self-Driving Cars 173

Appendix A: Teaching with this Material 185

Other Self-Driving Car Books by This Author 193

About the Author 255

Addendum 256

ACKNOWLEDGMENTS

I have been the beneficiary of advice and counsel by many friends, colleagues, family, investors, and many others. I want to thank everyone that has aided me throughout my career. I write from the heart and the head, having experienced first-hand what it means to have others around you that support you during the good times and the tough times.

To Warren Bennis, one of my doctoral advisors and ultimately a colleague, I offer my deepest thanks and appreciation, especially for his calm and insightful wisdom and support.

To Mark Stevens and his generous efforts toward funding and supporting the USC Stevens Center for Innovation.

To Lloyd Greif and the USC Lloyd Greif Center for Entrepreneurial Studies for their ongoing encouragement of founders and entrepreneurs.

To Peter Drucker, William Wang, Aaron Levie, Peter Kim, Jon Kraft, Cindy Crawford, Jenny Ming, Steve Milligan, Chis Underwood, Frank Gehry, Buzz Aldrin, Steve Forbes, Bill Thompson, Dave Dillon, Alan Fuerstman, Larry Ellison, Jim Sinegal, John Sperling, Mark Stevenson, Anand Nallathambi, Thomas Barrack, Jr., and many other innovators and leaders that I have met and gained mightily from doing so.

Thanks to Ed Trainor, Kevin Anderson, James Hickey, Wendell Jones, Ken Harris, DuWayne Peterson, Mike Brown, Jim Thornton, Abhi Beniwal, Al Biland, John Nomura, Eliot Weinman, John Desmond, and many others for their unwavering support during my career.

And most of all thanks as always to Lauren and Michael, for their ongoing support and for having seen me writing and heard much of this material during the many months involved in writing it. To their patience and willingness to listen.

INTRODUCTION

This is a book that provides the newest innovations and the latest Artificial Intelligence (AI) advances about the emerging nature of AI-based autonomous self-driving driverless cars. Via recent advances in Artificial Intelligence (AI) and Machine Learning (ML), we are nearing the day when vehicles can control themselves and will not require and nor rely upon human intervention to perform their driving tasks (or, that allow for human intervention, but only *require* human intervention in very limited ways).

Similar to my other related books, which I describe in a moment and list the chapters in the Appendix A of this book, I am particularly focused on those advances that pertain to self-driving cars. The phrase "autonomous vehicles" is often used to refer to any kind of vehicle, whether it is ground-based or in the air or sea, and whether it is a cargo hauling trailer truck or a conventional passenger car. Though the aspects described in this book are certainly applicable to all kinds of autonomous vehicles, I am focused more so here on cars.

Indeed, I am especially known for my role in aiding the advancement of self-driving cars, serving currently as the Executive Director of the Cybernetic AI Self-Driving Cars Institute.. In addition to writing software, designing and developing systems and software for self-driving cars, I also speak and write quite a bit about the topic. This book is a collection of some of my more advanced essays. For those of you that might have seen my essays posted elsewhere, I have updated them and integrated them into this book as one handy cohesive package.

You might be interested in companion books that I have written that provide additional key innovations and fundamentals about self-driving cars. Those books are entitled **"Introduction to Driverless Self-Driving Cars,"** "**Advances in AI and Autonomous Vehicles: Cybernetic Self-Driving Cars,**" "**Self-Driving Cars: "The Mother of All AI Projects," "Innovation and Thought Leadership on Self-Driving Driverless Cars," "New Advances in AI Autonomous Driverless Self-Driving Cars," "Autonomous Vehicle Driverless Self-Driving Cars and Artificial Intelligence," "Transformative Artificial Intelligence**

Driverless Self-Driving Cars," "Disruptive Artificial Intelligence and Driverless Self-Driving Cars, and **"State-of-the-Art AI Driverless Self-Driving Cars,"** and **"Top Trends in AI Self-Driving Cars,"** and **"AI Innovations and Self-Driving Cars," "Crucial Advances for AI Driverless Cars," "Sociotechnical Insights and AI Driverless Cars," "Pioneering Advances for AI Driverless Cars"** and **"Leading Edge Trends for AI Driverless Cars," "The Cutting Edge of AI Autonomous Cars"** and **"The Next Wave of AI Self-Driving Cars"** and **"Revolutionary Innovations of AI Self-Driving Cars,"** and **"AI Self-Driving Cars Breakthroughs," "Trailblazing Trends for AI Self-Driving Cars," "Ingenious Strides for AI Driverless Cars," "AI Self-Driving Cars Inventiveness," "Visionary Secrets of AI Driverless Cars," "Spearheading AI Self-Driving Cars," "Spurring AI Self-Driving Cars," "Avant-Garde AI Driverless Cars," "AI Self-Driving Cars Evolvement," "AI Driverless Cars Chrysalis," "Boosting AI Autonomous Cars," "AI Self-Driving Cars Trendsetting,"** and **"AI Autonomous Cars Forefront"** (they are all available via Amazon). Appendix A has a listing of the chapters covered.

For the introduction herein to this book, I am going to borrow my introduction from those companion books, since it does a good job of laying out the landscape of self-driving cars and my overall viewpoints on the topic. The remainder of the book is all new material that does not appear in the companion books.

INTRODUCTION TO SELF-DRIVING CARS

This is a book about self-driving cars. Someday in the future, we'll all have self-driving cars and this book will perhaps seem antiquated, but right now, we are at the forefront of the self-driving car wave. Daily news bombards us with flashes of new announcements by one car maker or another and leaves the impression that within the next few weeks or maybe months that the self-driving car will be here. A casual non-technical reader would assume from these news flashes that in fact we must be on the cusp of a true self-driving car. Here's a real news flash: We are still quite a distance from having a true self-driving car. It is years to go before we get there.

Why is that? Because a true self-driving car is akin to a moonshot. In the same manner that getting us to the moon was an incredible feat, likewise is achieving a true self-driving car. Anybody that suggests or even brashly states that the true self-driving car is nearly here should be viewed with great skepticism. Indeed, you'll see that I often tend to use the word "hogwash" or "crock" when I assess much of the decidedly ***fake news*** about self-driving cars.

Indeed, I've been writing a popular blog post about self-driving cars and hitting hard on those that try to wave their hands and pretend that we are on the imminent verge of true self-driving cars. For many years, I've been known as the AI Insider. Besides writing about AI, I also develop AI software. I do what I describe. It also gives me insights into what others that are doing AI are really doing versus what it is said they are doing.

Many faithful readers had asked me to pull together my insightful short essays and put them into another book, which you are now holding.

For those of you that have been reading my essays over the years, this collection not only puts them together into one handy package, I also updated the essays and added new material. For those of you that are new to the topic of self-driving cars and AI, I hope you find these essays approachable and informative. I also tend to have a writing style with a bit of a voice, and so you'll see that I am times have a wry sense of humor and poke at conformity.

As a former professor and founder of an AI research lab, I for many years wrote in the formal language of academic writing. I published in referred journals and served as an editor for several AI journals. This writing here is not of the nature, and I have adopted a different and more informal style for these essays. That being said, I also do mention from time-to-time more rigorous material on AI and encourage you all to dig into those deeper and more formal materials if so interested.

I am also an AI practitioner. This means that I write AI software for a living. Currently, I head-up the Cybernetics Self-Driving Car Institute, where we are developing AI software for self-driving cars. I am excited to also report that my son, also a software engineer, heads-up our Cybernetics Self-Driving Car Lab. What I have helped to start, and for which he is an integral part, ultimately he will carry long into the future after I have retired. My daughter, a marketing whiz, also is integral to our efforts as head of our Marketing group. She too will carry forward the legacy now being formulated.

For those of you that are reading this book and have a penchant for writing code, you might consider taking a look at the open source code available for self-driving cars. This is a handy place to start learning how to develop AI for self-driving cars. There are also many new educational courses spring forth. There is a growing body of those wanting to learn about and develop self-driving cars, and a growing body of colleges, labs, and other avenues by which you can learn about self-driving cars.

This book will provide a foundation of aspects that I think will get you ready for those kinds of more advanced training opportunities. If you've already taken those classes, you'll likely find these essays especially interesting as they offer a perspective that I am betting few other instructors or faculty offered to you. These are challenging essays that ask you to think beyond the conventional about self-driving cars.

THE MOTHER OF ALL AI PROJECTS

In June 2017, Apple CEO Tim Cook came out and finally admitted that Apple has been working on a self-driving car. As you'll see in my essays, Apple was enmeshed in secrecy about their self-driving car efforts. We have only been able to read the tea leaves and guess at what Apple has been up to. The notion of an iCar has been floating for quite a while, and self-driving engineers and researchers have been signing tight-lipped Non-Disclosure Agreements (NDA's) to work on projects at Apple that were as shrouded in mystery as any military invasion plans might be.

Tim Cook said something that many others in the Artificial Intelligence (AI) field have been saying, namely, the creation of a self-driving car has got to be the mother of all AI projects. In other words, it is in fact a tremendous moonshot for AI. If a self-driving car can be crafted and the AI works as we hope, it means that we have made incredible strides with AI and that therefore it opens many other worlds of potential breakthrough accomplishments that AI can solve.

Is this hyperbole? Am I just trying to make AI seem like a miracle worker and so provide self-aggrandizing statements for those of us writing the AI software for self-driving cars? No, it is not hyperbole. Developing a true self-driving car is really, really, really hard to do. Let me take a moment to explain why. As a side note, I realize that the Apple CEO is known for at times uttering hyperbole, and he had previously said for example that the year 2012 was "the mother of all years," and he had said that the release of iOS 10 was "the mother of all releases" – all of which does suggest he likes to use the handy "mother of" expression. But, I assure you, in terms of true self-driving cars, he has hit the nail on the head. For sure.

When you think about a moonshot and how we got to the moon, there are some identifiable characteristics and those same aspects can be applied to creating a true self-driving car. You'll notice that I keep putting the word "true" in front of the self-driving car expression. I do so because as per my essay about the various levels of self-driving cars, there are some self-driving cars that are only somewhat of a self-driving car. The somewhat versions are ones that require a human driver to be ready to intervene. In my view, that's not a true self-driving car. A true self-driving car is one that requires no human driver intervention at all. It is a car that can entirely undertake via automation the driving task without any human driver needed. This is the essence of what is known as a Level 5 self-driving car. We are currently at the Level 2 and Level 3 mark, and not yet at Level 5.

Getting to the moon involved aspects such as having big stretch goals, incremental progress, experimentation, innovation, and so on. Let's review how this applied to the moonshot of the bygone era, and how it applies to the self-driving car moonshot of today.

Big Stretch Goal

Trying to take a human and deliver the human to the moon, and bring them back, safely, was an extremely large stretch goal at the time. No one knew whether it could be done. The technology wasn't available yet. The cost was huge. The determination would need to be fierce. Etc. To reach a Level 5 self-driving car is going to be the same. It is a big stretch goal. We can readily get to the Level 3, and we are able to see the Level 4 just up ahead, but a Level 5 is still an unknown as to if it is doable. It should eventually be doable and in the same way that we thought we'd eventually get to the moon, but when it will occur is a different story.

Incremental Progress

Getting to the moon did not happen overnight in one fell swoop. It took years and years of incremental progress to get there. Likewise for self-driving cars. Google has famously been striving to get to the Level 5, and pretty much been willing to forgo dealing with the intervening levels, but most of the other self-driving car makers are doing the incremental route. Let's get a good Level 2 and a somewhat Level 3 going. Then, let's improve the Level 3 and get a somewhat Level 4 going. Then, let's improve the Level 4 and finally arrive at a Level 5. This seems to be the prevalent way that we are going to achieve the true self-driving car.

Experimentation

You likely know that there were various experiments involved in perfecting the approach and technology to get to the moon. As per making incremental progress, we first tried to see if we could get a rocket to go into space and safety return, then put a monkey in there, then with a human, then we went all the way to the moon but didn't land, and finally we arrived at the mission that actually landed on the moon. Self-driving cars are the same way. We are doing simulations of self-driving cars. We do testing of self-driving cars on private land under controlled situations. We do testing of self-driving cars on public roadways, often having to meet regulatory requirements including for example having an engineer or equivalent in the car to take over the controls if needed. And so on. Experiments big and small are needed to figure out what works and what doesn't.

Innovation

There are already some advances in AI that are allowing us to progress toward self-driving cars. We are going to need even more advances. Innovation in all aspects of technology are going to be required to achieve a true self-driving car. By no means do we already have everything in-hand that we need to get there. Expect new inventions and new approaches, new algorithms, etc.

Setbacks

Most of the pundits are avoiding talking about potential setbacks in the progress toward self-driving cars. Getting to the moon involved many setbacks, some of which you never have heard of and were buried at the time so as to not dampen enthusiasm and funding for getting to the moon. A recurring theme in many of my included essays is that there are going to be setbacks as we try to arrive at a true self-driving car. Take a deep breath and be ready. I just hope the setbacks don't completely stop progress. I am sure that it will cause progress to alter in a manner that we've not yet seen in the self-driving car field. I liken the self-driving car of today to the excitement everyone had for Uber when it first got going. Today, we have a different view of Uber and with each passing day there are more regulations to the ride sharing business and more concerns raised. The darling child only stays a darling until finally that child acts up. It will happen the same with self-driving cars.

SELF-DRIVING CARS CHALLENGES

But what exactly makes things so hard to have a true self-driving car, you might be asking. You have seen cruise control for years and years. You've lately seen cars that can do parallel parking. You've seen YouTube videos of Tesla drivers that put their hands out the window as their car zooms along the highway, and seen to therefore be in a self-driving car. Aren't we just needing to put a few more sensors onto a car and then we'll have in-hand a true self-driving car? Nope.

Consider for a moment the nature of the driving task. We don't just let anyone at any age drive a car. Worldwide, most countries won't license a driver until the age of 18, though many do allow a learner's permit at the age of 15 or 16. Some suggest that a younger age would be physically too small to reach the controls of the car. Though this might be the case, we could easily adjust the controls to allow for younger aged and thus smaller stature. It's not their physical size that matters. It's their cognitive development that matters.

To drive a car, you need to be able to reason about the car, what the car can and cannot do. You need to know how to operate the car. You need to know about how other cars on the road drive. You need to know what is allowed in driving such as speed limits and driving within marked lanes. You need to be able to react to situations and be able to avoid getting into accidents. You need to ascertain when to hit your brakes, when to steer clear of a pedestrian, and how to keep from ramming that motorcyclist that just cut you off.

Many of us had taken courses on driving. We studied about driving and took driver training. We had to take a test and pass it to be able to drive. The point being that though most adults take the driving task for granted, and we often "mindlessly" drive our cars, there is a significant amount of cognitive effort that goes into driving a car. After a while, it becomes second nature. You don't especially think about how you drive, you just do it. But, if you watch a novice driver, say a teenager learning to drive, you suddenly realize that there is a lot more complexity to it than we seem to realize.

Furthermore, driving is a very serious task. I recall when my daughter and son first learned to drive. They are both very conscientious people. They wanted to make sure that whatever they did, they did well, and that they did not harm anyone. Every day, when you get into a car, it is probably around 4,000 pounds of hefty metal and plastics (about two tons), and it is a lethal weapon. Think about it. You drive down the street in an object that weighs two tons and with the engine it can accelerate and ram into anything you want to hit. The damage a car can inflict is very scary. Both my children were surprised that they were being given the right to maneuver this monster of a beast that could cause tremendous harm entirely by merely letting go of the steering wheel for a moment or taking your eyes off the road.

In fact, in the United States alone there are about 30,000 deaths per year by auto accidents, which is around 100 per day. Given that there are about 263 million cars in the United States, I am actually more amazed that the number of fatalities is not a lot higher. During my morning commute, I look at all the thousands of cars on the freeway around me, and I think that if all of them decided to go zombie and drive in a crazy maniac way, there would be many people dead. Somehow, incredibly, each day, most people drive relatively safely. To me, that's a miracle right there. Getting millions and millions of people to be safe and sane when behind the wheel of a two ton mobile object, it's a feat that we as a society should admire with pride.

So, hopefully you are in agreement that the driving task requires a great deal of cognition. You don't' need to be especially smart to drive a car, and we've done quite a bit to make car driving viable for even the average dolt. There isn't an IQ test that you need to take to drive a car. If you can read and write, and pass a test, you pretty much can legally drive a car. There are of course some that drive a car and are not legally permitted to do so, plus there are private areas such as farms where drivers are young, but for public roadways in the United States, you can be generally of average intelligence (or less) and be able to legally drive.

This though makes it seem like the cognitive effort must not be much. If the cognitive effort was truly hard, wouldn't we only have Einstein's that could drive a car? We have made sure to keep the driving task as simple as we can, by making the controls easy and relatively standardized, and by having roads that are relatively standardized, and so on. It is as though Disneyland has put their Autopia into the real-world, by us all as a society agreeing that roads will be a certain way, and we'll all abide by the various rules of driving.

A modest cognitive task by a human is still something that stymies AI. You certainly know that AI has been able to beat chess players and be good at other kinds of games. This type of narrow cognition is not what car driving is about. Car driving is much wider. It requires knowledge about the world, which a chess playing AI system does not need to know. The cognitive aspects of driving are on the one hand seemingly simple, but at the same time require layer upon layer of knowledge about cars, people, roads, rules, and a myriad of other "common sense" aspects. We don't have any AI systems today that have that same kind of breadth and depth of awareness and knowledge.

As revealed in my essays, the self-driving car of today is using trickery to do particular tasks. It is all very narrow in operation. Plus, it currently assumes that a human driver is ready to intervene. It is like a child that we have taught to stack blocks, but we are needed to be right there in case the child stacks them too high and they begin to fall over. AI of today is brittle, it is narrow, and it does not approach the cognitive abilities of humans. This is why the true self-driving car is somewhere out in the future.

Another aspect to the driving task is that it is not solely a mind exercise. You do need to use your senses to drive. You use your eyes a vision sensors to see the road ahead. You vision capability is like a streaming video, which your brain needs to continually analyze as you drive. Where is the road? Is there a pedestrian in the way? Is there another car ahead of you? Your senses are relying a flood of info to your brain. Self-driving cars are trying to do the same, by using cameras, radar, ultrasound, and lasers. This is an attempt at mimicking how humans have senses and sensory apparatus.

Thus, the driving task is mental and physical. You use your senses, you use your arms and legs to manipulate the controls of the car, and you use your brain to assess the sensory info and direct your limbs to act upon the controls of the car. This all happens instantly. If you've ever perhaps gotten something in your eye and only had one eye available to drive with, you suddenly realize how dependent upon vision you are. If you have a broken foot with a cast, you suddenly realize how hard it is to control the brake pedal and the accelerator. If you've taken medication and your brain is maybe sluggish, you suddenly realize how much mental strain is required to drive a car.

An AI system that plays chess only needs to be focused on playing chess. The physical aspects aren't important because usually a human moves the chess pieces or the chessboard is shown on an electronic display. Using AI for a more life-and-death task such as analyzing MRI images of patients, this again does not require physical capabilities and instead is done by examining images of bits.

Driving a car is a true life-and-death task. It is a use of AI that can easily and at any moment produce death. For those colleagues of mine that are developing this AI, as am I, we need to keep in mind the somber aspects of this. We are producing software that will have in its virtual hands the lives of the occupants of the car, and the lives of those in other nearby cars, and the lives of nearby pedestrians, etc. Chess is not usually a life-or-death matter.

Driving is all around us. Cars are everywhere. Most of today's AI applications involve only a small number of people. Or, they are behind the scenes and we as humans have other recourse if the AI messes up. AI that is driving a car at 80 miles per hour on a highway had better not mess up. The consequences are grave. Multiply this by the number of cars, if we could put magically self-driving into every car in the USA, we'd have AI running in the 263 million cars. That's a lot of AI spread around. This is AI on a massive scale that we are not doing today and that offers both promise and potential peril.

There are some that want AI for self-driving cars because they envision a world without any car accidents. They envision a world in which there is no car congestion and all cars cooperate with each other. These are wonderful utopian visions.

They are also very misleading. The adoption of self-driving cars is going to be incremental and not overnight. We cannot economically just junk all existing cars. Nor are we going to be able to affordably retrofit existing cars. It is more likely that self-driving cars will be built into new cars and that over many years of gradual replacement of existing cars that we'll see the mix of self-driving cars become substantial in the real-world.

In these essays, I have tried to offer technological insights without being overly technical in my description, and also blended the business, societal, and economic aspects too. Technologists need to consider the non-technological impacts of what they do. Non-technologists should be aware of what is being developed.

We all need to work together to collectively be prepared for the enormous disruption and transformative aspects of true self-driving cars. We all need to be involved in this mother of all AI projects.

WHAT THIS BOOK PROVIDES

What does this book provide to you? It introduces many of the key elements about self-driving cars and does so with an AI based perspective. I weave together technical and non-technical aspects, readily going from being concerned about the cognitive capabilities of the driving task and how the technology is embodying this into self-driving cars, and in the next breath I discuss the societal and economic aspects.

They are all intertwined because that's the way reality is. You cannot separate out the technology per se, and instead must consider it within the milieu of what is being invented and innovated, and do so with a mindset towards the contemporary mores and culture that shape what we are doing and what we hope to do.

WHY THIS BOOK

I wrote this book to try and bring to the public view many aspects about self-driving cars that nobody seems to be discussing.

For business leaders that are either involved in making self-driving cars or that are going to leverage self-driving cars, I hope that this book will enlighten you as to the risks involved and ways in which you should be strategizing about how to deal with those risks.

For entrepreneurs, startups and other businesses that want to enter into the self-driving car market that is emerging, I hope this book sparks your interest in doing so, and provides some sense of what might be prudent to pursue.

For researchers that study self-driving cars, I hope this book spurs your interest in the risks and safety issues of self-driving cars, and also nudges you toward conducting research on those aspects.

For students in computer science or related disciplines, I hope this book will provide you with interesting and new ideas and material, for which you might conduct research or provide some career direction insights for you.

For AI companies and high-tech companies pursuing self-driving cars, this book will hopefully broaden your view beyond just the mere coding and development needed to make self-driving cars.

For all readers, I hope that you will find the material in this book to be stimulating. Some of it will be repetitive of things you already know. But I am pretty sure that you'll also find various eureka moments whereby you'll discover a new technique or approach that you had not earlier thought of. I am also betting that there will be material that forces you to rethink some of your current practices.

I am not saying you will suddenly have an epiphany and change what you are doing. I do think though that you will reconsider or perhaps revisit what you are doing.

For anyone choosing to use this book for teaching purposes, please take a look at my suggestions for doing so, as described in the Appendix. I have found the material handy in courses that I have taught, and likewise other faculty have told me that they have found the material handy, in some cases as extended readings and in other instances as a core part of their course (depending on the nature of the class).

In my writing for this book, I have tried carefully to blend both the practitioner and the academic styles of writing. It is not as dense as is typical academic journal writing, but at the same time offers depth by going into the nuances and trade-offs of various practices.

The word "deep" is in vogue today, meaning getting deeply into a subject or topic, and so is the word "unpack" which means to tease out the underlying aspects of a subject or topic. I have sought to offer material that addresses an issue or topic by going relatively deeply into it and make sure that it is well unpacked.

In any book about AI, it is difficult to use our everyday words without having some of them be misinterpreted. Specifically, it is easy to anthropomorphize AI. When I say that an AI system "knows" something, I do not want you to construe that the AI system has sentience and "knows" in the same way that humans do. They aren't that way, as yet. I have tried to use quotes around such words from time-to-time to emphasize that the words I am using should not be misinterpreted to ascribe true human intelligence to the AI systems that we know of today. If I used quotes around all such words, the book would be very difficult to read, and so I am doing so judiciously. Please keep that in mind as you read the material, thanks.

Some of the material is time-based in terms of covering underway activities, and though some of it might decay, nonetheless I believe you'll find the material useful and informative.

COMPANION BOOKS

1. **"Introduction to Driverless Self-Driving Cars"** by Dr. Lance Eliot
2. **"Innovation and Thought Leadership on Self-Driving Driverless Cars"** by Dr. Lance Eliot
3. **"Advances in AI and Autonomous Vehicles: Cybernetic Self-Driving Cars"** by Dr. Lance Eliot
4. **"Self-Driving Cars: The Mother of All AI Projects"** by Dr. Lance Eliot
5. **"New Advances in AI Autonomous Driverless Self-Driving Cars"** by Dr. Lance Eliot
6. **"Autonomous Vehicle Driverless Self-Driving Cars and Artificial Intelligence"** by Dr. Lance Eliot and Michael B. Eliot
7. **"Transformative Artificial Intelligence Driverless Self-Driving Cars"** by Dr. Lance Eliot
8. **"Disruptive Artificial Intelligence and Driverless Self-Driving Cars"** by Dr. Lance Eliot
9. **"State-of-the-Art AI Driverless Self-Driving Cars"** by Dr. Lance Eliot
10. **"Top Trends in AI Self-Driving Cars"** by Dr. Lance Eliot
11. **"AI Innovations and Self-Driving Cars"** by Dr. Lance Eliot
12. **"Crucial Advances for AI Driverless Cars"** by Dr. Lance Eliot
13. **"Sociotechnical Insights and AI Driverless Cars"** by Dr. Lance Eliot.
14. **"Pioneering Advances for AI Driverless Cars"** by Dr. Lance Eliot
15. **"Leading Edge Trends for AI Driverless Cars"** by Dr. Lance Eliot
16. **"The Cutting Edge of AI Autonomous Cars"** by Dr. Lance Eliot
17. **"The Next Wave of AI Self-Driving Cars"** by Dr. Lance Eliot
18. **"Revolutionary Innovations of AI Driverless Cars"** by Dr. Lance Eliot
19. **"AI Self-Driving Cars Breakthroughs"** by Dr. Lance Eliot
20. **"Trailblazing Trends for AI Self-Driving Cars"** by Dr. Lance Eliot
21. **"Ingenious Strides for AI Driverless Cars"** by Dr. Lance Eliot
22. **"AI Self-Driving Cars Inventiveness"** by Dr. Lance Eliot
23. **"Visionary Secrets of AI Driverless Cars"** by Dr. Lance Eliot
24. **"Spearheading AI Self-Driving Cars"** by Dr. Lance Eliot
25. **"Spurring AI Self-Driving Cars"** by Dr. Lance Eliot
26. **"Avant-Garde AI Driverless Cars"** by Dr. Lance Eliot
27. **"AI Self-Driving Cars Evolvement"** by Dr. Lance Eliot
28. **"AI Driverless Cars Chrysalis"** by Dr. Lance Eliot
29. **"Boosting AI Autonomous Cars"** by Dr. Lance Eliot
30. **"AI Self-Driving Cars Trendsetting"** by Dr. Lance Eliot
31. **"AI Autonomous Cars Forefront"** by Dr. Lance Eliot

These books are available on Amazon and at other major global booksellers.

CHAPTER 1

ELIOT FRAMEWORK FOR AI SELF-DRIVING CARS

CHAPTER 1

ELIOT FRAMEWORK FOR AI SELF-DRIVING CARS

This chapter is a core foundational aspect for understanding AI self-driving cars and I have used this same chapter in several of my other books to introduce the reader to essential elements of this field. Once you've read this chapter, you'll be prepared to read the rest of the material since the foundational essence of the components of autonomous AI driverless self-driving cars will have been established for you.

When I give presentations about self-driving cars and teach classes on the topic, I have found it helpful to provide a framework around which the various key elements of self-driving cars can be understood and organized (see diagram at the end of this chapter). The framework needs to be simple enough to convey the overarching elements, but at the same time not so simple that it belies the true complexity of self-driving cars. As such, I am going to describe the framework here and try to offer in a thousand words (or more!) what the framework diagram itself intends to portray.

The core elements on the diagram are numbered for ease of reference. The numbering does not suggest any kind of prioritization of the elements. Each element is crucial. Each element has a purpose, and otherwise would not be included in the framework. For some self-driving cars, a particular element might be more important or somehow distinguished in comparison to other self-driving cars.

You could even use the framework to rate a particular self-driving car, doing so by gauging how well it performs in each of the elements of the framework. I will describe each of the elements, one at a time. After doing so, I'll discuss aspects that illustrate how the elements interact and perform during the overall effort of a self-driving car.

At the Cybernetic Self-Driving Car Institute, we use the framework to keep track of what we are working on, and how we are developing software that fills in what is needed to achieve Level 5 self-driving cars.

D-01: Sensor Capture

Let's start with the one element that often gets the most attention in the press about self-driving cars, namely, the sensory devices for a self-driving car.

On the framework, the box labeled as D-01 indicates "Sensor Capture" and refers to the processes of the self-driving car that involve collecting data from the myriad of sensors that are used for a self-driving car. The types of devices typically involved are listed, such as the use of mono cameras, stereo cameras, LIDAR devices, radar systems, ultrasonic devices, GPS, IMU, and so on.

These devices are tasked with obtaining data about the status of the self-driving car and the world around it. Some of the devices are continually providing updates, while others of the devices await an indication by the self-driving car that the device is supposed to collect data. The data might be first transformed in some fashion by the device itself, or it might instead be fed directly into the sensor capture as raw data. At that point, it might be up to the sensor capture processes to do transformations on the data. This all varies depending upon the nature of the devices being used and how the devices were designed and developed.

D-02: Sensor Fusion

Imagine that your eyeballs receive visual images, your nose receives odors, your ears receive sounds, and in essence each of your distinct sensory devices is getting some form of input. The input befits the nature of the device. Likewise, for a self-driving car, the cameras provide visual images, the radar returns radar reflections, and so on.

Each device provides the data as befits what the device does.

At some point, using the analogy to humans, you need to merge together what your eyes see, what your nose smells, what your ears hear, and piece it all together into a larger sense of what the world is all about and what is happening around you. Sensor fusion is the action of taking the singular aspects from each of the devices and putting them together into a larger puzzle.

Sensor fusion is a tough task. There are some devices that might not be working at the time of the sensor capture. Or, there might some devices that are unable to report well what they have detected. Again, using a human analogy, suppose you are in a dark room and so your eyes cannot see much. At that point, you might need to rely more so on your ears and what you hear. The same is true for a self-driving car. If the cameras are obscured due to snow and sleet, it might be that the radar can provide a greater indication of what the external conditions consist of.

In the case of a self-driving car, there can be a plethora of such sensory devices. Each is reporting what it can. Each might have its difficulties. Each might have its limitations, such as how far ahead it can detect an object. All of these limitations need to be considered during the sensor fusion task.

D-03: Virtual World Model

For humans, we presumably keep in our minds a model of the world around us when we are driving a car. In your mind, you know that the car is going at say 60 miles per hour and that you are on a freeway. You have a model in your mind that your car is surrounded by other cars, and that there are lanes to the freeway. Your model is not only based on what you can see, hear, etc., but also what you know about the nature of the world. You know that at any moment that car ahead of you can smash on its brakes, or the car behind you can ram into your car, or that the truck in the next lane might swerve into your lane.

The AI of the self-driving car needs to have a virtual world model, which it then keeps updated with whatever it is receiving from the sensor fusion, which received its input from the sensor capture and the sensory devices.

D-04: System Action Plan

By having a virtual world model, the AI of the self-driving car is able to keep track of where the car is and what is happening around the car. In addition, the AI needs to determine what to do next. Should the self-driving car hit its brakes? Should the self-driving car stay in its lane or swerve into the lane to the left? Should the self-driving car accelerate or slow down?

A system action plan needs to be prepared by the AI of the self-driving car. The action plan specifies what actions should be taken. The actions need to pertain to the status of the virtual world model. Plus, the actions need to be realizable.

This realizability means that the AI cannot just assert that the self-driving car should suddenly sprout wings and fly. Instead, the AI must be bound by whatever the self-driving car can actually do, such as coming to a halt in a distance of X feet at a speed of Y miles per hour, rather than perhaps asserting that the self-driving car come to a halt in 0 feet as though it could instantaneously come to a stop while it is in motion.

D-05: Controls Activation

The system action plan is implemented by activating the controls of the car to act according to what the plan stipulates. This might mean that the accelerator control is commanded to increase the speed of the car. Or, the steering control is commanded to turn the steering wheel 30 degrees to the left or right.

One question arises as to whether or not the controls respond as they are commanded to do. In other words, suppose the AI has commanded the accelerator to increase, but for some reason it does not do so. Or, maybe it tries to do so, but the speed of the car does not increase. The controls activation feeds back into the virtual world model, and simultaneously the virtual world model is getting updated from the sensors, the sensor capture, and the sensor fusion. This allows the AI to ascertain what has taken place as a result of the controls being commanded to take some kind of action.

By the way, please keep in mind that though the diagram seems to have a linear progression to it, the reality is that these are all aspects of the self-driving car that are happening in parallel and simultaneously. The sensors are capturing data, meanwhile the sensor fusion is taking place, meanwhile the virtual model is being updated, meanwhile the system action plan is being formulated and reformulated, meanwhile the controls are being activated.

This is the same as a human being that is driving a car. They are eyeballing the road, meanwhile they are fusing in their mind the sights, sounds, etc., meanwhile their mind is updating their model of the world around them, meanwhile they are formulating an action plan of what to do, and meanwhile they are pushing their foot onto the pedals and steering the car. In the normal course of driving a car, you are doing all of these at once. I mention this so that when you look at the diagram, you will think of the boxes as processes that are all happening at the same time, and not as though only one happens and then the next.

They are shown diagrammatically in a simplistic manner to help comprehend what is taking place. You though should also realize that they are working in parallel and simultaneous with each other. This is a tough aspect in that the inter-element communications involve latency and other aspects that must be taken into account. There can be delays in one element updating and then sharing its latest status with other elements.

D-06: Automobile & CAN

Contemporary cars use various automotive electronics and a Controller Area Network (CAN) to serve as the components that underlie the driving aspects of a car. There are Electronic Control Units (ECU's) which control subsystems of the car, such as the engine, the brakes, the doors, the windows, and so on.

The elements D-01, D-02, D-03, D-04, D-05 are layered on top of the D-06, and must be aware of the nature of what the D-06 is able to do and not do.

D-07: In-Car Commands

Humans are going to be occupants in self-driving cars. In a Level 5 self-driving car, there must be some form of communication that takes place between the humans and the self-driving car. For example, I go into a self-driving car and tell it that I want to be driven over to Disneyland, and along the way I want to stop at In-and-Out Burger. The self-driving car now parses what I've said and tries to then establish a means to carry out my wishes.

In-car commands can happen at any time during a driving journey. Though my example was about an in-car command when I first got into my self-driving car, it could be that while the self-driving car is carrying out the journey that I change my mind. Perhaps after getting stuck in traffic, I tell the self-driving car to forget about getting the burgers and just head straight over to the theme park. The self-driving car needs to be alert to in-car commands throughout the journey.

D-08: V2X Communications

We will ultimately have self-driving cars communicating with each other, doing so via V2V (Vehicle-to-Vehicle) communications. We will also have self-driving cars that communicate with the roadways and other aspects of the transportation infrastructure, doing so via V2I (Vehicle-to-Infrastructure).

The variety of ways in which a self-driving car will be communicating with other cars and infrastructure is being called V2X, whereby the letter X means whatever else we identify as something that a car should or would want to communicate with. The V2X communications will be taking place simultaneous with everything else on the diagram, and those other elements will need to incorporate whatever it gleans from those V2X communications.

D-09: Deep Learning

The use of Deep Learning permeates all other aspects of the self-driving car. The AI of the self-driving car will be using deep learning to do a better job at the systems action plan, and at the controls activation, and at the sensor fusion, and so on.

Currently, the use of artificial neural networks is the most prevalent form of deep learning. Based on large swaths of data, the neural networks attempt to "learn" from the data and therefore direct the efforts of the self-driving car accordingly.

D-10: Tactical AI

Tactical AI is the element of dealing with the moment-to-moment driving of the self-driving car. Is the self-driving car staying in its lane of the freeway? Is the car responding appropriately to the controls commands? Are the sensory devices working?

For human drivers, the tactical equivalent can be seen when you watch a novice driver such as a teenager that is first driving. They are focused on the mechanics of the driving task, keeping their eye on the road while also trying to properly control the car.

D-11: Strategic AI

The Strategic AI aspects of a self-driving car are dealing with the larger picture of what the self-driving car is trying to do. If I had asked that the self-driving car take me to Disneyland, there is an overall journey map that needs to be kept and maintained.

There is an interaction between the Strategic AI and the Tactical AI. The Strategic AI is wanting to keep on the mission of the driving, while the Tactical AI is focused on the particulars underway in the driving effort. If the Tactical AI seems to wander away from the overarching mission, the Strategic AI wants to see why and get things back on track. If the Tactical AI realizes that there is something amiss on the self-driving car, it needs to alert the Strategic AI accordingly and have an adjustment to the overarching mission that is underway.

D-12: Self-Aware AI

Very few of the self-driving cars being developed are including a Self-Aware AI element, which we at the Cybernetic Self-Driving Car Institute believe is crucial to Level 5 self-driving cars.

The Self-Aware AI element is intended to watch over itself, in the sense that the AI is making sure that the AI is working as intended. Suppose you had a human driving a car, and they were starting to drive erratically. Hopefully, their own self-awareness would make them realize they themselves are driving poorly, such as perhaps starting to fall asleep after having been driving for hours on end. If you had a passenger in the car, they might be able to alert the driver if the driver is starting to do something amiss. This is exactly what the Self-Aware

AI element tries to do, it becomes the overseer of the AI, and tries to detect when the AI has become faulty or confused, and then find ways to overcome the issue.

D-13: Economic

The economic aspects of a self-driving car are not per se a technology aspect of a self-driving car, but the economics do indeed impact the nature of a self-driving car. For example, the cost of outfitting a self-driving car with every kind of possible sensory device is prohibitive, and so choices need to be made about which devices are used. And, for those sensory devices chosen, whether they would have a full set of features or a more limited set of features.

We are going to have self-driving cars that are at the low-end of a consumer cost point, and others at the high-end of a consumer cost point. You cannot expect that the self-driving car at the low-end is going to be as robust as the one at the high-end. I realize that many of the self-driving car pundits are acting as though all self-driving cars will be the same, but they won't be. Just like anything else, we are going to have self-driving cars that have a range of capabilities. Some will be better than others. Some will be safer than others. This is the way of the real-world, and so we need to be thinking about the economics aspects when considering the nature of self-driving cars.

D-14: Societal

This component encompasses the societal aspects of AI which also impacts the technology of self-driving cars. For example, the famous Trolley Problem involves what choices should a self-driving car make when faced with life-and-death matters. If the self-driving car is about to either hit a child standing in the roadway, or instead ram into a tree at the side of the road and possibly kill the humans in the self-driving car, which choice should be made?

We need to keep in mind the societal aspects will underlie the AI of the self-driving car. Whether we are aware of it explicitly or not, the AI will have embedded into it various societal assumptions.

D-15: Innovation

I included the notion of innovation into the framework because we can anticipate that whatever a self-driving car consists of, it will continue to be innovated over time. The self-driving cars coming out in the next several years will undoubtedly be different and less innovative than the versions that come out in ten years hence, and so on.

Framework Overall

For those of you that want to learn about self-driving cars, you can potentially pick a particular element and become specialized in that aspect. Some engineers are focusing on the sensory devices. Some engineers focus on the controls activation. And so on. There are specialties in each of the elements.

Researchers are likewise specializing in various aspects. For example, there are researchers that are using Deep Learning to see how best it can be used for sensor fusion. There are other researchers that are using Deep Learning to derive good System Action Plans. Some are studying how to develop AI for the Strategic aspects of the driving task, while others are focused on the Tactical aspects.

A well-prepared all-around software developer that is involved in self-driving cars should be familiar with all of the elements, at least to the degree that they know what each element does. This is important since whatever piece of the pie that the software developer works on, they need to be knowledgeable about what the other elements are doing.

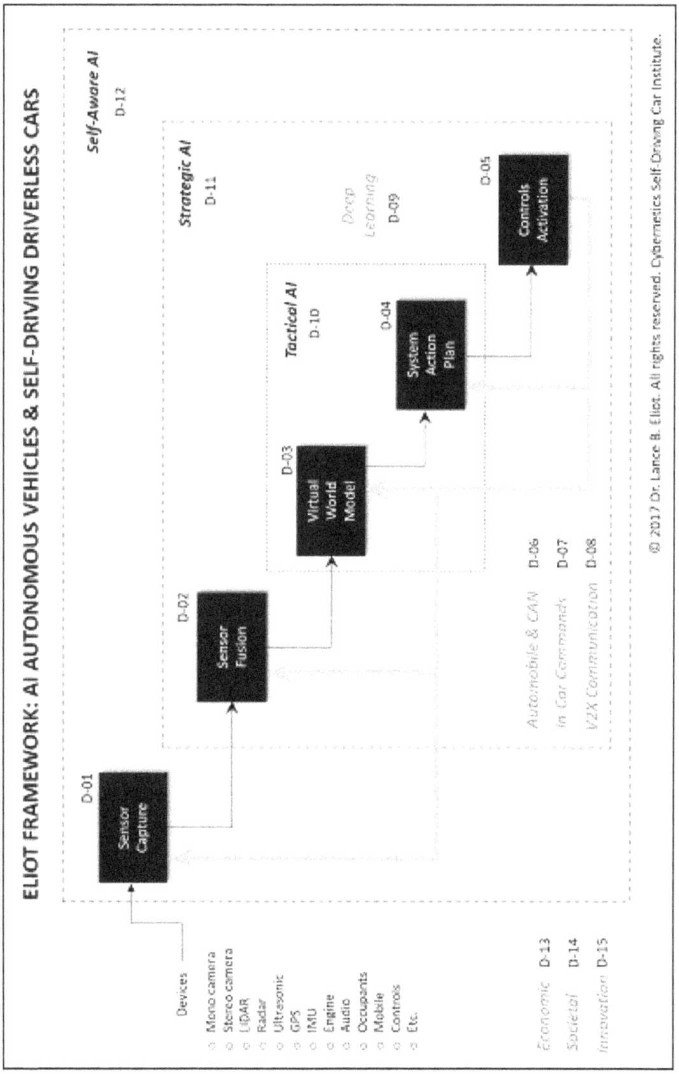
ELIOT FRAMEWORK: AI AUTONOMOUS VEHICLES & SELF-DRIVING DRIVERLESS CARS
Self-Aware AI
D-12
Strategic AI
D-11
Tactical AI
D-10
Sensor Capture
D-01
Sensor Fusion
D-02
Virtual World Model
D-03
System Action Plan
D-04
Controls Activation
D-05
Deep Learning
D-09
Automobile & CAN D-06
In Car Commands D-07
V2X Communication D-08
Devices
Mono camera
Stereo camera
LIDAR
Radar
Ultrasonic
GPS
IMU
Engine
Audio
Occupants
Mobile
Controls
Etc.
Economic D-13
Societal D-14
Innovation D-15
© 2017 Dr. Lance B. Eliot. All rights reserved. Cybernetics Self-Driving Car Institute.

CHAPTER 2
ESSENTIAL STATS AND AI SELF-DRIVING CARS

CHAPTER 2
ESSENTIAL STATS AND AI SELF-DRIVING CARS

In speaking at various industry events, I am often asked about some of the various stats frequently mentioned as a form of justification or rationale for the pursuit of autonomous driverless cars. At times, such stats are batted around, and it is hard to know where they came from, nor know whether they are reliable, and often these "magical" numbers are inappropriately utilized.

You might at first thought believe that autonomous cars don't especially need any kind of numeric or quantitative justification. It would seem obvious to assume that driverless cars are going to be a boon to society, some would assert. In a qualitative manner, self-driving driverless cars will presumably expand mobility throughout society, unlocking the sometimes costly or arduous, some say friction-based, access to daily transportation. That's enough to convince many that we are on the right path by seeking to develop and field autonomous cars.

There is a rub.

The path to achieving driverless cars is not going to be quite as easy as some might suggest. For example, society currently appears to be reactive to any kind of injury or death involving an autonomous car, and yet proponents of driverless cars are quick to point out that conventional car injuries and deaths are happening each and every day.

Why should we get upset when an autonomous car happens to do something that human based driving is already doing?

Indeed, some are worried that if society is only going to permit some kind of roadway perfection as the standard bearer, it means that we would likely need to stop all autonomous car tryouts on our public roadways. Meanwhile, automakers and tech firms say that without public roadway tryouts, and if only confined to using proving grounds or closed tracks, and using simulations, the odds are that it will take a lot longer to arrive at autonomous cars, possibly never getting there at all.

Furthermore, if the lack of public roadway tryouts delayed the advent of autonomous cars, it could be argued that such a self-imposed delay is actually costing lives.

How so?

With today's conventional cars, there are daily deaths. The longer that we go without autonomous cars, the more deaths will continue during the interim period. Thus, in a facts-based cost-benefit analysis, one could say that you would be trading off some deaths possibly now, during the "imperfect" era of autonomous cars as they are getting "perfected" (let's be clear, there isn't going to be perfection in the sense of zero deaths by autonomous cars, as I have exhorted many times), but balanced against shortening the window of conventional car deaths while doing so.

The Big Unanswered Question Is How Safe Is Safe

This also raises another quite crucial question, namely, how safe is safe?

As alluded to in my remarks already, anyone believing that only zero deaths or zero injuries is the mark of readiness for autonomous cars would be living in a kind of dreamworld or Utopia.

We are going to have autonomous cars that get into car accidents, which can happen because something goes awry in the autonomous car (like encountering an AI software bug or hardware fault that is not otherwise caught), or because the car breaks down in some manner (remember, it's still a car, composed of mechanical and vulnerable to wear-and-tear on its parts), or due to say a pedestrian that unexpectedly leaps in front of an autonomous car for which the physics prevents the driverless car from avoiding the pedestrian, and so on.

Proponents of autonomous cars are often quick to step into such a discussion and point out that though those kinds of car accidents might indeed occur, it is presumed that this will happen with a lot less frequency than with today's conventional human driving.

And so, when trying to ascertain "how safe is safe" the use of today's statistics about conventional driving become very important. They are the baseline against which we might try to compare autonomous cars, doing so to find a balance between harm from autonomous car incidents versus the harm already underway by conventional human driving.

Statistics Tell A Difficult And Agonizing Story

It is hard to contemplate deaths and injuries in the abstract.

When I quote some of the stats that I am about to share with you, I find myself often cringing and am impacted by the numbers. Any death from car accidents is obviously one too many. Any injuries from car accidents is likewise abhorrent. That being said, the reality is that we live in a world wherein there is a presumed societal necessity of having cars, and inevitably there is going to be some amount of injuries or deaths involved.

Here's some crucial assumptions about these stats:

- **Sources Used.** As to the sources of the numbers that I am about to share with you, they by-and-large come from the National Highway Traffic Safety Administration (NHTSA), the National Transportation Safety Board (NTSB), the Census Bureau, the Center for Disease Control (CDC), and similar governmental and research bodies.

- **Focusing On The United States Herein.** For this set of stats, I'm focused solely on the United States, thus they are a country-specific set, which means that when you explore the numbers and when you make use of the numbers please treat them as such (do NOT try to extrapolate them to being global).

- **Forewarning: These Stats Are Only Order-Of-Magnitude.** Here's perhaps the hardest part for many, I am going to be using imprecise numbers that are approximations and offered primarily as an order-of-magnitude indication. I mention this facet because I'm sure that many of these numbers are changing as we speak, plus some of the numbers are older due to as-yet-updates provided by the sources. And so on. Do NOT consider these numbers and stats as the be-all end-all. Instead, consider them as overall approximations, providing sufficient general indications and not being pinpoint or exacting numbers. If you try to add-up some of these numbers, they won't come out to the exact mathematical total, and will instead at times be "reasonably" close to the totals. Many of the numbers are being rounded. Etc. This is maddening to some, but overall acceptable when trying to consider the big-picture aspects.

With those caveats and limitations in mind, let's unpack the stats.

U.S. Car Crash Approximated Deaths And Injuries

Here's the approximated deaths and injuries due to car accidents in the United States:

Per hour (for a 24-hour day): 4 deaths per hour
Per hour (for a 24-hour day): 285 injuries per hour

Per day: 100 deaths per day
Per day: 6,850 injured per day

Per week: 700 deaths per week
Per week: 48,000 injured per week

Per month: 3,000 deaths per month
Per month: 205,000 injured per month

Per year: 37,000 deaths per year
Per year: 2,500,000 injured per year

Ponder those stats. For some, their breath is taken away at the notion that there are approximately 37,000 human beings killed as a result of car accidents each year (now nearing 40,000). Staggering. Since the number 37,000 is difficult to fathom, I usually say that it is about 100 people per day. When I give a speech at a sizable conference room or hall, I point to an area of the audience that appears to be around 100 people, and I tell them that they showcase what a one hundred people looks like. It drives home the abysmal point.

By the way, the reason that the per hour indicates "for a 24-hour day" (as though there is something other than a 24-hour day that might be used), it is because most driving doesn't happen equally around the clock per se, and tends to be clumped or clustered in certain parts of the day, therefore the per hour should probably be higher than shown if you were to consider peak hours of the day, but it would maybe create confusion so I use just a conventional 24-hour basis.

The injured number of about 2 ½ million is somewhat "easy" to shrug off, since you might be thinking about bumps and bruises, but the injuries are typically reported more so when severe, often entirely debilitating and forever altering the lives of those injured. Take those numbers seriously.

U.S. Approximated Number Of Car Accidents

Here's the approximated number of car accidents or crashes in the United States:

Per hour (for a 24-hour day): 720 car crashes per hour
Per day: 17,260 car crashes per day
Per week: 120,000 car crashes per week
Per month: 518,000 car crashes per month
Per year: 6,300,000 car crashes per year

Ponder those stats. Each day, across the United States, there are approximately 17,260 car accidents or car crashes. Each day! It is hard to fathom. You can make use of these stats in combination with the other stats herein, though If so, be careful doing things like deciding to divide the number of car crashes by the number of states, which would give you a somewhat misleading indicator per state (misleading in that some states like California and New York are the dominant occurrences, while other less-populous states have a lower count).

U.S. Distance Traveled And Deaths/Injured/Crashes

Here's the number of miles traveled via car annually in the United States, along with the number of annual deaths and injured counts:

3.2T miles traveled annually / 37K deaths yearly = 86M miles traveled per each death

3.2T miles traveled annually / 2.5M injured yearly = 1.3M miles traveled per each injured

3.2T miles traveled annually / 6.3M car crashes yearly = 508K miles traveled per crash

Ponder those stats. These are important stats, since they are often used to compare to the track record of autonomous cars to-date. In essence, some use these to suggest that if an autonomous car appears to be incurring a car crash of say per every 508K miles it would seemingly be doing as well as human drivers, while if it did say 1.7M miles per each injury it would be seemingly doing better than human driving (since it went further along before incurring a crash). There are many problematic aspects about such a comparison.

One glaring aspect that makes such a comparison questionable is the number of miles actually traveled, such as if the autonomous cars have traveled only some several millions of miles (or even billions), it is a far cry from the trillions of miles being used as the "baseline" for comparative purposes. What is accomplished in a sprint is not necessarily logically extensible to what happens in a marathon.

U.S. Car Deaths By Mode Of Human Transport

Let's zoom-in and look more closely at the number of car related deaths (the 37,000 annually), doing so to see what the status of the human involved was:

Drivers deaths:	51% :	19,000 people
Passengers deaths:	17% :	6,200 people
Motorcyclists deaths:	15% :	5,500 people
Pedestrian deaths:	17% :	6,200 people

Ponder those stats. The deaths weight toward drivers, which makes sense in that currently there must a human driver in the car, and thus this stat includes situations whereby the driver is the only human in the car, along with circumstances of having passengers in the car. Also, the human driver is typically in a position in the car that is more likely to incur a death than say a passenger seated in the backseat of the car.

What is perhaps shockingly alarming is the motorcyclist deaths, which when you consider the number of licensed car drivers in the United States, which is about 225M, versus the around only 10M licensed motorcyclists, the stats showcase just how dangerous it is to be a motorcycle rider. Of course, the pedestrian deaths are also perhaps shocking too, though if you assume that at some point the entire U.S. population is acting as a pedestrian, and the population is around 325M, maybe the numbers for pedestrian deaths is not as high as you might anticipate. Again, all these deaths are abhorrent.

U.S. Annual Car Deaths By Approximated Cause

Let's once again look more closely at the number of car related deaths (the 37,000 annually), doing so to see what the approximated cause was of the car accident or crash that led to the deaths:

Drunk driving:	30% :	11,000 people
Speeding:	30% :	11,000 people
Distracted driving:	16% :	6,000 people
Weather:	22% :	8,000 people
Drowsy:	02% :	1,000 people

Ponder those stats: First, take these categories and counts with a solid dose of salt. A reported reason for a car crash that involved a death can widely vary and might not necessarily tell the whole story. If someone for example crashes in foul weather and a death occurs, and the weather is blamed as the cause, it could be that there was drowsiness that led to the driver not well coping with the weather yet the weather was listed as the cause, and so on.

In any case, one of the top reasons given to expedite transitioning to autonomous cars is that presumably an AI system is not going to get drunk and therefore won't be a drunk driver that gets into a deathly crash. If that's the case, presumably you'll be able to reduce the annual number of car related deaths by about one-third.

Likewise, some suggest that if autonomous cars are programmed to not speed, you'll presumably reduce another third. The AI shouldn't get drowsy, so that's 2% reduced from the list. Distracted driving should also be taken off the list. In that case, there's the 22% that remains due to weather, and the question will be whether or not the AI system would even try to drive in foul weather, or that it might actually be better at foul weather driving than humans.

There are some logical fallacies about this aspect, which I'll cover in a later column.

U.S. Causes Of Death Annually

One other useful stat involves considering how Americans are killed each year, doing so to compare the deaths from car accidents to the magnitude of other means of getting killed. Obviously, the 37,000 deaths is terrible and we need to find ways to reduce that number of deaths, but at the same time, it is instructive to look at where this fits into the various means of death (note: only selected types of death are shown in this chart, there are other categories and other counts):

Heart disease:	24.0% :	635,000 deaths per year
Tumors:	22.0% :	598,000 deaths per year
Respiratory disease	6.0% :	155,000 deaths per year
Accidental poisoning	2.5% :	65,000 deaths per year
Kidney disease	2.0% :	50,000 deaths per year
Car crash deaths	***1.4% :***	***37,000 deaths per year***
Hypertension	1.2%:	33,000 deaths per year
Parkinson's disease	1.1%:	30,000 deaths per year

Other causes of deaths (not shown) leading to a total of 2.7M deaths per year.

Ponder those stats. I know this will be hard to digest, but consider if you had limited resources and attention, and wanted to ascertain where best to put your efforts to reduce the annual number of deaths, where would you put those efforts?

I ask this question because some say that the monies going toward trying to reduce car crash deaths might be disproportionate to perhaps spending those same dollars to reduce heart disease deaths, which as you can see is many magnitudes larger in scope than car related deaths. Again, all deaths are dreadful. Anyway, there are arguments and counterarguments on all sides of this matter.

Conclusion

Some of you are likely already having heartburn about these numbers because you might know of more current counts, or you might not like how a particular number was rounded up or down, and so on. I'll repeat my earlier remarks that this is intended only as overarching order-of-magnitude uses, and you should see them in that light, and you should not quote or cite these numbers without also carrying along a similar precautionary indication about them.

Also, there are a slew of other stats and counts that are also pertinent (yes, I realize this), but I'm trying to keep this piece to a manageable and digestible size.

All told, I hope that this collection of some key stats will contribute to the ongoing dialogue about the advent of autonomous cars.

CHAPTER 3
STATS FALLACIES AND AI SELF-DRIVING CARS

CHAPTER 3

STATS FALLACIES AND AI SELF-DRIVING CARS

As I've previously mentioned in my writing and speeches, Tesla and Elon Musk's vision for the realization of semi-autonomous and fully autonomous cars is commendable and has undoubtedly helped spur progress on advancing toward achieving self-driving driverless cars. That being said, it is constructive to consider the nature of the statistics being provided to the public by both Tesla and Musk when it comes to asserting the miles-safety related triumphs they purport to have already accomplished.

Why try to unpack claims regarding miles-safety stats?

For both those within the autonomous car industry and those outside it, there needs to be a realistic understanding of what the existing semi-autonomous and autonomous car capabilities are, and so any time that any automaker or tech firm reports their stats, it is worthwhile to examine closely the provided numbers.

Let's be clear about my key axioms on this matter:

- No firm should be immune to such scrutiny.

- All autonomous car makers should be willing to share their stats and do so in a manner that offers a verifiable and veracious indication of their latest and ongoing status (referred to as "safety data transparency")

- And please be aware that I say this about any and all autonomous car developers and am not singling out Tesla per se and am preparing a series of columns as a likewise analysis of other driverless car makers.

Let's consider several important background aspects before we dig into the numbers.

Dangers Of Spreading Fake News About Autonomous Cars

Some point to the handful of states that require disengagements reporting as a seeming showcase depicting the autonomous car tryouts taking place on our public roadways (a "disengagement" is generally counted as an instance of a human back-up driver having to take over control of an autonomous car during public roadway tryouts, though there is a lot of wiggle room in the definition).

As I've indicated in my speeches and writings, those disengagement reports are not particularly revealing and nor a viable means to grasp and portray what the true status of the matter is.

Indeed, when the disengagement numbers are released by various governmental entities, there is often a flurry of news accounts about the statistics, a kind of unruly rush-to-judgment to meet the voracious news-cycle demand, yet if the media promulgating those numbers took a moment to carefully dissect the figures, they'd be doing a much better job of informing the public in a more rightful manner.

We need to try and curtail the rise of fake news about autonomous cars, which I've been decrying for several years now as a widening malady.

Unfortunately, at times the media merely passes along the reported stats and inoculates the numbers with an impression that the counts must be forthright and revealing, yet that often is not the case. Don't though mistake my remarks as meaning that I am suggesting that we should abandon such reporting, I am simply asserting that regrettably the nature of the metrics used and how they are being reported is essentially weak and somewhat vapid, and I've exhorted that more robust metrics need to be put in place and offered suggestions thereof.

Tesla and Musk have already been reproached about some of their prior roadway safety claims, perhaps most notably when the National Highway Traffic Safety Administration (NHTSA) finally released data that took a federal lawsuit to get into the public's hands, and showcased that the previously and widely touted 40% claimed reduction in crash rates by Tesla's introduction of their Autosteer feature was not quite up-to-par. Analysts characterized the claims as "implausible" and not supportable by the data, and others even used the more profane word of "bogus" after reviewing the data.

Tesla Quarterly Miles-Safety Data Reports

Starting in October of last year, Tesla began reporting what they describe as quarterly safety data, doing so at their publicly accessible web site. When you hear that it is "quarterly safety data" you might be inclined to assume that it is a slew of detailed data that provides a richness of information, making available a plethora of safety data for public consumption.

Not quite.

Essentially, it is a single paragraph that has two numbers reported, consisting of the purported number of miles driven prior to a car accident or crash occurs, shown as one number for the case of Autopilot engaged and a second number of when a Tesla car was being driven without Autopilot engaged.

That's it.

For those wishing to do any kind of analysis about safety related aspects of Tesla cars, the providing merely of two numbers could be characterized as a paucity of data (some would use harsher wording).

In brief:

- There is no indication of the means by which Tesla arrived at the two numbers.
- There is no apparent means for anyone to verify the veracity of the two numbers.
- There is no underlying data provided that could be used in furtherance of interpreting the numbers.
- There aren't any other numbers other than the two numbers, but for which there certainly are many other stats that they could provide, given that they are able to provide these two numbers.
- There would not seem to be any additional effort or cost that Tesla would incur to provide additional data or additional stats, since presumably they are already doing so for their own internal purposes.
- There would not seem to be any qualm or concern about somehow revealing any proprietary aspects by releasing more so stats or underlying data, since it can be readily done without divulging any technology or IP (Intellectual Property) they might rightfully wish to keep private.
- Etc.

Be that as it may, let's see what those two numbers are and how Tesla to-date has made claims about them as an indicator of the Tesla cars mile-safety track record.

Reported Tesla Numbers And What They Mean

Here's the reported numbers (for clarity, these aren't my numbers, these are the Tesla reported numbers) and for which the sole metric is stated as being one car accident or crash-like event per number of miles driven:

Q1 2019: 2.87M miles driven in which Autopilot was engaged
Q1 2019: 1.76M miles driven without Autopilot engaged

Q4 2018: 2.91M miles driven in which Autopilot was engaged
Q4 2018: 1.58M miles driven without Autopilot engaged

Q3 2018: 3.34M miles driven in which Autopilot was engaged
Q3 2018: 1.92M miles driven without Autopilot engaged

Another way to group the numbers would be by showing them over time and whether in the Autopilot engaged or not engaged case:

Q1 2019: 2.87M miles driven in which Autopilot was engaged
Q4 2018: 2.91M miles driven in which Autopilot was engaged
Q3 2018: 3.34M miles driven in which Autopilot was engaged

Q1 2019: 1.76M miles driven without Autopilot engaged
Q4 2018: 1.58M miles driven without Autopilot engaged
Q3 2018: 1.92M miles driven without Autopilot engaged

So, what do these stats mean?

First, keep in mind that the higher the number the better things are, in the sense that it implies that the longer or more miles a car went prior to getting into a car accident or crash. Theoretically, you would never want any car accidents or car crashes, in which case we might aim for the value of infinity, which I say in some jest, but the point being that the goal is to maximize the magnitude of the miles driven before there is a car crash that occurs.

You might have noticed that the numbers when the Autopilot was not engaged are less than the numbers when Autopilot is engaged. This implies that the Autopilot engaged grouping goes further along before incurring a car crash, or you can also consider that it means the grouping without Autopilot engaged gets into a car crash in a lesser distance traveled than those of the Autopilot engaged grouping.

As an aside, one somewhat small point but worth mentioning involves the group that involves the "without engaged" Autopilot portion. Presumably, this includes Tesla's that have Autopilot but for which the Autopilot was not engaged for some portion of traveling and thus those count as not-engaged miles (you might drive on a single journey of 60 miles, going 10 miles while using Autopilot, and in that same journey not use Autopilot for say 50 miles, and therefore rack-up 10 miles into the Autopilot engaged group and 50 miles into the "without engaged" group). Also, a Tesla without Autopilot available would presumably only rack-up miles into the "without engaged" group, by definition.

For ease of comparison between the Autopilot engaged group and the not-engaged Autopilot grouping, the average for the Autopilot engaged is mathematically 3.04 and the grouping without Autopilot engaged is 1.75, by simple math, and you could suggest that therefore the Autopilot engaged group is about two times the distance before a car crash occurs (actually being about 1.7x, rounded to the number 2).

If you look at the numbers over time, you'll notice that the Autopilot engaged group did "better" in Q3 2018, but then appeared to drop by about 13% in Q4 2018 (in a sense, worsening), and then further dropping another 1-2% for Q1 2019.

You'll likely also notice that for the without-Autopilot engaged group, it dropped (worsened) from Q3 2018 to Q4 2018 by decreasing about 18%, and then somewhat rebounded for Q1 2019 (improving from Q4 2018 but still below Q3 2018)

Some have made a bit of a ruckus about the fluctuations in the stats, but I'm not going to entertain that aspect herein, trying also to keep this article to a manageable size (though I do have some thoughts about it!).

Plus, I think there is bigger fish to be considered.

Possible Claims Based On The Tesla Reported Numbers

Within the paragraphs posted by Tesla, they indicate that the NHTSA nationwide data indicate that nationally there is a car crash every 436K miles (in Q1 2019 and likewise for Q4 2018) and was 492K in Q3 2018.

As such, this suggests that the average distance of the Autopilot engaged group of 3.04M miles per crash is presumably much greater (better) than the national average of cars overall (about 7x), and the average distance of the Autopilot not engaged of 1.75M miles is also presumably greater (better) than the national average though somewhat less so than when the Autopilot was engaged (about 4x versus the 7x), implying that overall, the Tesla cars are going longer distances before incurring a car crash than the national average – as earlier mentioned, the larger the miles driven before incurring a car crash is something considered desirable.

In any case, here's what seems to be the preponderance of the overall claims sometimes made about these particular stats:

- Claim #1: On a comparative basis, the use of Autopilot versus not using Autopilot appears to presumably indicate that the driving task is being undertaken on a safer basis when the Autopilot is engaged (since we have that 1.7x or rounded to 2x greater distance traveled prior to a car crash).

- Claim #2: On a comparative basis, the Tesla cars are presumably being driven on a safer basis overall since the Autopilot engaged group miles-to-crash is larger than the national average miles-to-crash (by about 7x), and so is the not-engaged Autopilot group higher than the national average of miles-safety driven (by about 4x).

There are pundits in the autonomous car industry that like to latch onto the first claim as it suggests that autonomous cars are safer than non-autonomous cars, but this is a quite misleading and a false interpretation, I assert. Keep in mind that Tesla cars are not fully autonomous as yet, they are at a Level 2, rather than a truly autonomous Level 5, thus this is only about semi-autonomous cars, ones that involve a co-sharing of the driving task by human and machine, rather than the machine or AI being the sole driver of the car.

Given that caveat, some pundits will then back-down to saying that it at least "shows" or "demonstrates" that using semi-autonomous capabilities leads to safer driving (since, on a comparative basis, the Autopilot engaged group seems to go a greater distance before incurring a car crash than the not-engaged Autopilot group).

There are a number of potential statistical fallacies involved in these kinds of proclamations, and it would be instructive to reveal those potential fallacies.

Statistical Fallacies Of Interpreting The Safety-Miles Stats

When I was a university professor, I taught AI classes and also often taught statistics courses too, since it turns out that statistics are an important element in AI areas such as Machine Learning, Deep Learning, and probabilistic reasoning. One of the required readings for my students was the best-selling book "How To Lie with Statistics" that was written by Darrell Huff and has stood the test of time in terms of laying out some of the most commonly misunderstood aspects about interpreting statistics.

Studies show over and again that people often fall into numerous mental traps when interpreting statistical data and are vulnerable to statistical fallacies.

Here's an example. I ask five people to wear regular shoes to play a basketball game against five other people that are wearing specialized basketball-playing sports shoes. After playing a fierce basketball game, the team wearing the specialized sports shoes wins. What might you conclude? I'm sure that most would believe that the specialized sports shoes made the difference in terms of why the one team beat the other team, having been given an added edge attributed to those sporty shoes.

But suppose I then told you that the team wearing regular shoes were only allowed to make shots from beyond the free-throw line, while the other team could make shots anywhere and including right next to the basket. Whoa! You might now change your mind and say that it wasn't particularly the shoes that made the difference.

For the Claim #1, namely that the use of Autopilot appears to have led to greater safety since the miles-safety distance stat is larger than the group that did not have Autopilot engaged, your likely first impression is that it must be the Autopilot usage that led to safer driving.

But, hold-on a moment, and let's think about that, maybe there's a statistical fallacy lurking in that thinking.

Please be aware that in the autonomous car industry, it is well-known that not all miles are the same, meaning that if you put an autonomous car onto a wide open highway with minimal traffic, it is a lot easier for the AI than if you put that same autonomous car into a dense city setting that is chock full of traffic, pesky pedestrians, and other "car accident" inducing elements.

Here's the question for you, when the Autopilot is being engaged, what is the nature of the roadway driving involved? Is it more likely that the miles racked-up while on Autopilot are on the highways rather than in other settings? Does this potentially suggest that we might be comparing apples and oranges? Similar to the story about the basketball team, our attention might be focused on the shoes (i.e., Autopilot), when it could be that the type of miles being driven when Autopilot is engaged are less so likely to incur car crashes.

If Tesla would provide the underlying data, anonymized for privacy protection, it would be possible to potentially analyze to see what type of driving areas are used for Autopilot engagement, and then possibly find a comparable subset of data of the not-engaged Autopilot data to see whether those are showcasing differences (it would be a more suitable basis for comparison, though we might still have additional confounding or underlying factors).

Overall, it would be best to cautiously consider the claim #1 as "we don't know" whether it really portends any significant difference due to the use of Autopilot, rather than trying to leap to a brazen or unsubstantiated conclusion.

For Claim #2, there is a somewhat similar potential statistical fallacy involved.

Returning to the basketball teams, I bring forth a third team, wearing just regular shoes. I make the basketball game rules all equal, meaning you can shoot from anyplace on the court that you prefer. The team with the specialized shoes handily beats this new team, and furthermore the other team that had only regular shoes also beats this third team. Why? Turns out that initial two teams were composed of college basketball players, while the third team was a hodgepodge of people that just happened to be around when composing the third team.

In Claim #2, it appears that the Tesla with Autopilot engaged drivers are safer than the nationwide driver car crash stat, and so too is the Tesla without Autopilot engaged drivers. Does this mean that somehow Tesla cars are safer than all other cars? We have no reasonable way to make that conclusion.

Keep in mind that Tesla's tend to be more expensive cars to-date, aiming toward a luxury line, and the buyers are demographically likely a niche, differing from everyday drivers per se. Furthermore, Tesla buyers are generally considered "early adopters" which is yet another kind of niche or slice of everyday drivers, wherein the masses or "late adopters" have not yet become Tesla drivers.

It could be that the type of driver that is driving Tesla cars is unlike the overall mix of all drivers that is reflected in the national miles-to-crash statistic. In that sense, it could be that the driver is the difference, rather than the car itself.

Or, maybe Tesla cars are primarily being driven in areas of the country that are not representative of the driving encompassed by the national stat, thus, perchance the Tesla cars are being driven in places that tend toward having less car crashes or car crashes at longer intervals of driving.

And so on, there are lots of other potential intervening elements that makes the comparison problematic, which again if the data was available it would allow for a closer analysis to try and see whether those other factors could be examined.

Plus, there is oftentimes a big difference between being able to achieve an effort in a shorter run versus a longer run, pointing out that the distance annually traveled by all cars in the U.S. is about 3.2T, which is what the national stat is based upon, while as far as has been reported to-date it might be that Tesla cars have been driven perhaps 10B miles (thus, a mere fraction of the overall national driving distance). Running a sprint versus running a marathon can produce quite difference results when trying to compare the running times and stats.

Conclusion

Correlation does not imply causation, it's a key mantra for anyone that is versed in statistics and statistical reasoning. We all tend to assume that whenever we see stats that they are based on some kind of random sampling and that any intervening variables are being controlled (this rigorous setup usually happens when performing a laboratory-based experiment or similar kinds of more statistically planned research efforts).

Mark Twain was famous for popularizing a quip: "There are three kinds of lies: lies, dammed lies, and statistics." It is important that any stats that are provided by any automaker or tech firm about their semi-autonomous or autonomous cars be carefully scrutinized and not be inappropriately interpreted or utilized.

CHAPTER 4

DRIVER BULLIES AND AI SELF-DRIVING CARS

CHAPTER 4
DRIVER BULLIES AND AI SELF-DRIVING CARS

The official California DMV Driver Handbook provides prescribed driving practices that everyone is supposed to comply with while driving on our state roadways, including topics such as safe driving methods when the roads are wet from rain (admittedly, we don't get much rain, but when we do, California drivers are known to freak-out and drive crazily), and driving when there is a tough curve or when on a a steep hill, plus what to do when driving nearby animal-drawn vehicles or coming up to railroad tracks.

There are over 130 pages of crucial material in our DMV Driver Handbook, which licensed California drivers get tested on and presumably need to understand and are expected to obey (alright, I acknowledge that many don't, but without those explicitly "you are on notice" regs, I think we'd agree that there might be chaos or at least even worse driving exploits than we already experience).

Furthermore, the booklet is chockfull of stern warnings about how you can get a moving violation ticket or get charged with other kinds of criminal infractions, and potentially have your license revoked, if you don't drive in a proper manner as codified in the laws and regulations stipulated in the California Vehicle Code (CVC).

Here's a question for you to consider: Should the state handbooks on licensed driving include prescribed practices for human drivers to abide by when they are driving nearby to self-driving driverless autonomous cars?

Some say yes, namely that we need to update our myriad of state driving handbooks, and correspondingly each of the state sets of vehicle codes, so as to include specifics about expectations for human drivers when traffic-wise encountering autonomous cars. The logic being that since there are already explicitly stated expectations about driving nearby to motorcyclists, nearby to bicyclists, nearby to horse-drawn carriages, there ought to be a similar inclusion about driving nearby to driverless cars.

Those that say no, meaning that they don't see a need to include driving practices depicting autonomous cars as a special roadway consideration for human drivers, argue that an autonomous car should be treated as any other car being driven on our streets and highways. In essence, they insist that the existing driving regulations are sufficient, and that human drivers are to drive in the same manner that they drive when around other human drivers; thus, in this viewpoint, it makes no difference whether a car happens to be driven by a human or an AI system. Treat them all the same, they would contend.

What The Fuss Is All About

You might be somewhat perplexed on this subject because there are pundits that keep predicting that we'll have only autonomous cars on our roadways and the human driving act will become as extinct as the dodo bird.

Imagine a world in which all cars are driverless cars. No need to worry about the wild antics of human drivers. No need to license human drivers.

No longer pine away about distracted driving, drunk driving, and the other sad and dangerous driving larks that contribute to our annually disheartening car crash death rates and injuries. Instead, AI "drivers" will be whisking us to-and-fro, and presumably communicating with each other, via V2V (vehicle-to-vehicle electronic communications), ensuring that they don't step on each other's toes or get into traffic bogs.

Let's set the record straight on this aspect.

For the foreseeable future, we'll have a mixture of human driven cars and AI-driven cars, and it won't be some overnight transformation that we suddenly have all and only autonomous cars on our roadways. In the United States alone, there are over 250 million conventional cars and they aren't going to disappear simply due to the emergence of self-driving cars. Presumably, driverless cars will gradually be introduced, slowly and gradually increasing in numbers, which will likely lead to a gradual decreasing of human driven cars, all of this taking place over many decades to come.

In addition, there is an open question about whether or not we'll ever fully get rid of human driving, which some argue that human driving should always be retained for those that wish to drive (claiming it is a right, but I'll gently point out it is actually considered a privilege and not a right per se), plus concerns that if we don't allow human driving then humans will become deskilled at the driving task, apparently alluding to the idea that we will become dependent and subservient to AI systems (a conspiracy theory that driverless cars are part of an elaborate AI-takeover plot).

Anyway, let's for now agree that there will be a time period during which human drivers and AI self-driving cars will be on our roads together. Will they play nicely with each other?

For AI developers, they are struggling with getting autonomous cars to gauge what human drivers do. There are AI developers that whine about the pesky human drivers and the sloppy and perilous driving tricks that humans employ while at the steering wheel of a car. It's a lot easier to setup an AI system to drive a car when there aren't human drivers in the mix of traffic. If we could somehow ban all human driving, it is presumed that we'd already have autonomous cars galore on our streets (or, at least be getting much closer to doing so).

Exploitation By Human Drivers Of Nearby Driverless Cars

There are two facets about the nature of human drivers that need to get considered in this matter:

1. Human drivers driving in their everyday questionable ways, and then perchance are doing so while nearby autonomous cars.

2. Human drivers realizing that an autonomous car is nearby, and purposely aiming to maneuver in a manner intended to play with, confound, overrule, or otherwise exploit the driverless car.

Many of the automakers and tech firms that are developing and starting to field public roadway tryouts of their autonomous cars are generally trying to deal with the first facet already. Earlier versions of driverless cars might have been coded in a fashion that the AI assumed there weren't human drivers around, but the latest versions tend to be aiming to deal with human drivers that are nearby and that are (hopefully) driving in a normally human way, including being an commonplace greedy driver, being an uncaring driver, being a reckless driver, and so on.

The second facet is a bit of twist on this topic, and one that has not yet gotten much attention.

For the second facet, human drivers are at times changing their driving behavior specifically and explicitly when they encounter an autonomous car. You might liken this to what some human drivers do when they see a novice teenager driving a car that's marked as a driver instruction vehicle. Believe it or not, some human drivers do rather dastardly things toward such a vehicle.

For example, some "seasoned" drivers try to cutoff the novice teenage driver, wanting to see how the neophyte will handle it. I suppose you could say it is a kind of experiment, perhaps driven by curiosity, wanting to gauge the reaction of the novice teenage driver. Other times a weathered driver might zip around the novice teenage driver, doing so because the novice is going no faster than the speed limit, and the zipping past driver has no time to waste and gets exasperated at trailing behind the so-called slowpoke. And so on.

In case you weren't already aware, human drivers are now starting to do that same kind of "triggered" driving whenever they see that an autonomous car is nearby.

It's usually pretty easy to spot an autonomous car, either due to the sensors protruding from the car, or sometimes the car has a branding message on the side that tells you it is a driverless car, or it could be that there's no human in the driver's seat (there is nearly always so far a human back-up driver in the car, sitting at the driver's seat, thus, it would appear to be human driven, though sometimes the back-up driver might be seated in the backseat and be using auxiliary driving controls).

During your first-ever encounter with an autonomous car, doing so when you are driving nearby it, your reaction usually involves a kind of open-mouthed gapping fascination of what you are seeing, but, since these tryouts are typically occurring in the same geo-fenced areas, over and over again, you eventually get more accustomed to seeing these driverless cars.

Apparently, with familiarity comes a bit of disdain.

Some like to cutoff the driverless car and see what happens, akin to the same trickery pulled on a novice teenage driver. Others are annoyed that the self-driving car is abiding by the speed limit and do the zip around maneuver to leave the autonomous car in the dust. There are pranks being played on self-driving cars, such as coming up to a four-way stop, and the human driver seizing the right-of-way by rolling through the stop sign, meanwhile the driverless car waits patiently because it has been coded to only take its dutiful turn when so permitted (even if it reached the stop sign first).

Conclusion

How shall we as a society contend with these human drivers that want to prank the AI systems of driverless cars?

Merely telling people to stop their hunger-games efforts is not likely to do much. I think we all realize that human behavior on a societal scale is arduous to adjust and shift.

Here's some more armed options that have been voiced:

- **Make it the law.** Put into the official driving regulations in each state that any such driving acts by human drivers against or toward an autonomous car is against the law.

By explicitly naming autonomous cars as a kind of protected class, as it were, this might get human drivers to be more accommodating. At least it would allow for clearly having provided a forewarning (otherwise those offending human drivers might say they didn't know it was wrong to do such acts toward an autonomous car, if you buy into that kind of rather vacuous argument), and make those human drivers legally susceptible to getting a ticket or losing their human driving privileges.

- **Catch the scofflaws.** Since human drivers know they can get away with these dreadful driving antics and not likely get caught (you can't have traffic police on every corner), consider using the sensory data collected by autonomous cars as a means to legally pursue the untoward human drivers.

Keep in mind that autonomous cars will have cameras capturing whatever is visually happening around the driverless car. Perhaps the recorded video could be uploaded to your local police station that would then examine it and if a human driver did something wrong, a ticket would be issued and ultimately after enough violations their driver's license revoked. This approach though has a lot of privacy concerns and other contentious elements to it, so don't place your bets on this option for happening anytime soon.

- **Divide up our roads.** Perhaps it is best to not have human drivers mixing with autonomous cars, and thus we could divide up our roads, having some streets or highways, or particular lanes, declared as for human driven cars only and others for autonomous cars only.

The notion of dividing the roads is fraught with all kinds of problematic issues. The odds are that the cost to do this would be enormous. Is that really the best way to spend our limited infrastructure dollars? Also, some worry that this is a short-term fix not worthy of investment, and that if indeed human driving is going to winnow down, time will solve this conundrum.

- **Toughen up the AI.** This viewpoint says that autonomous cars ought to be able to drive in the same way that other humans drive, fighting fire-with-fire, so to speak.

If a human driver is going to be aggressive toward an autonomous car, the driverless car shouldn't necessarily backdown (bowing to the human bully), and instead needs to showcase that it too is willing to play the dog-eat-dog driving game.

This will presumably "teach" human drivers not to mess with autonomous cars, and overtime society will adjust to allowing autonomous cars the same driving "courtesies" as they do among other humans.

Some worry though that if we toughen up the AI, we will have self-driving cars that will start driving in the same untoward manner that humans do. We'll wake-up one morning and find ourselves confronted by "angry" AI systems that dare human drivers, in the same way that human drivers do, which could indeed be a consequence of Machine Learning, whereby the AI has merely mimicked driving behavior patterns based on the collected driving of how human drivers antagonistically maneuver.

One wonders, would bullying by AI driverless systems get those human drivers that we all already despise to become reborn as civil and polite drivers? If so, maybe it would be worth having slightly aggressive autonomous cars. Or, would we only end-up with lots more car accidents, road rages by human drivers against those in-your-face AI systems, and fail to gain the hoped-for reductions in car crash related deaths and injuries?

We're in the midst of placing a new set of "drivers" onto our roadways, and we need to figure out how the existing drivers will deal with these strangers, perhaps welcoming them with open arms or instead exploiting them like they are newbies that deserve a hazing.

CHAPTER 5
SUNDAY DRIVES AND AI SELF-DRIVING CARS

CHAPTER 5
SUNDAY DRIVES AND AI SELF-DRIVING CARS

The revered pastime of going for a Sunday drive.

When I was a kid, my parents only had one car for the family and my father used that automotive workhorse to drive to work each day. This meant that during the weekdays, our only source of automotive capability was by-and-large unavailable to the rest of us and meanwhile sat in a parking lot at my dad's workplace some 25 miles away.

I'm not complaining, mind you, and merely indicating that the only time that the family car was around consisted mainly of the weekends. Our cherished car usually went unused on Saturdays, one might say it was a day of rest for the car, since us kids were involved in sports at the walking-distance sports fields and there wasn't a need to use the car to get there, even though the vaunted machine was available for family use.

Come Sunday afternoons, my parents would often announce that we were to clamor into the car and we'd all go for a drive. I know this sounds rather quaint, and perhaps old-fashioned (tracing back to the 1920's and 1930s, but I assure you I'm not that old), yet I must say that it became a treasured pastime and something that we kids all tremendously relished.

Of course, the Sunday drives that society used to undertake have gradually neared extinction.

Some say it was a waste of limited resources and needlessly used up gasoline. Others point out that the Sunday drive was emitting pollution when there's no valid basis for using an emissions laden car engine. There have even been religious arguments that Sunday drives, if undertaken for the mere act of driving around, were potentially not in proper abidance to faith principles that are to be observed on Sundays. And so on.

It is claimed that Henry Ford was a staunch and outspoken advocate of people going for a Sunday drive, which seemingly was a bit of self-promotion for the selling of his newfangled cars, one might argue. And yet, maybe it worked because today there is an average of about 2.28 cars per household, and this ratio gets further boosted by the aspect that around one-third of households have three or more cars.

You could interpret these stats as meaning that it would be easier to therefore go for a leisurely Sunday drive, but another seemingly more likely interpretation is that there is no longer an impetus to go for a Sunday drive per se. In essence, overall, people have enough cars to get around throughout the week, and the novelty of going for a drive is no longer there, partially due to the plentiful availability of the car as a resource.

Don't misunderstand my statement, I'm not suggesting that we have sufficient cars available for all, and nor that we have too many cars, I'm just pointing out that the novelty factor of actually getting into and going for a ride is not what it used to be. As a related aside, I am reminded of going for plane travels as a child on our vacation trips, and my parents got us dressed-up to do so, due to the aspect at that time that flying was a novelty. Today, I think we can all agree that flying is a commoditized and generally plentiful resource, allowing for masses to use airborne travel methods (my most recent flight from NYC to LAX had all manner of attire by the travelers, which I assure you did not especially tip the dressing-in-style scale).

Here's a question to consider: Will the advent of autonomous cars bring back the bygone tradition of going for a Sunday drive?

I'm betting that you might at first glance be perplexed that autonomous cars would have anything to do with Sunday driving and might summarily reject the proposition that somehow the advent of self-driving driverless cars would impact Sunday driving in any manner.

Read on.

Autonomous Cars Become Ridesharing Money Makers

Most pundits would assert that the advent of autonomous cars will lead to an expansive boon in ridesharing.

When I refer to autonomous cars, I am talking about a truly autonomous car, ones that do not require a human licensed driver, typically known as a Level 5 (a Level 4 is somewhat similar but allows for the AI to not have to be able to drive in all circumstances that a human could drive a car, which limits therefore its full utility).

For ridesharing purposes, a fully autonomous car is quite handy since it implies that a car can be available all of the time, 24x7, seven days a week (other than during maintenance time, etc.). It is like having a non-stop driver that is willing to take you wherever you want to go. Via a mobile app, you'll be able to request a ride, an autonomous car shows-up, you ride to your destination, and the autonomous car then seeks another rider, doing this repeatedly, without the "driver" needing any rest or break in the driving effort.

Some believe that the cost of owning an autonomous car will be so high that only large companies will be able to afford them and then offer the driverless cars as a ridesharing service to the public.

I've been a proponent for many years that there is a solid chance that individuals will seek to own autonomous cars, doing so to try and make some money on-the-side of their normal job (while sitting at work, your autonomous car is performing ridesharing and earning you "extra" monies on the side). Today's conventional car ownership is not a money-maker scheme (you "lose" money), while with autonomous cars the potential for having a viable means to boost your income will spur a cottage industry of individuals owning and leveraging their driverless cars, I contend.

I realize that my prediction about individual car ownership in an era of plentiful autonomous cars has some controversy associated with it, but for my Sunday driving argument it is not a necessary condition, as you'll see in a moment.

Breaking Up The Family And So Bringing It Back Together

Okay, so let's envision that autonomous cars are whisking people around via ridesharing.

Currently, most of the driving or at least the consumption of driving efforts occurs during the weekdays, and the weekends are statistically portrayed as lesser driving days of the week. I suppose this makes logical sense that the weekdays, when we need to get to work and get to school, would be likely to involve driving or automotive travel more so than on the weekends when those needs are lessened.

I'm going to assume that the same pattern will continue into the future, unaffected by the rise of driverless cars.

During weekdays, you and your family members are all making use of autonomous cars, let's say mainly via ridesharing, and can each go your own ways, since you don't need an adult licensed driver. You might send the kids off to school in the morning, bereft of you as the parent having to drive them there.

In fact, there are some indications that as a family unit, we won't be traveling together as much when using autonomous cars, instigated by the lack of needing an adult licensed driver in the car. Today, parents pretty much "must" ferry around their kids. In the future, no need to do so, just have the AI system do the driving and the autonomous car shelps the kids wherever you want them to be.

When the weekend arrives, I'll bet that Saturdays are going to continue to be hectic days for the voluminous extracurricular activities of modern-day on-the-go kids. Studies showcase that the children of today are often booked and overbooked with back-to-back efforts on Saturdays, including sports, piano lessons, recitals, college readying study sessions, meditation sessions (well, some do this), and a plethora of over-achieving FOMO (fear of missing out) cavalcade of efforts and duties.

Aha, I've now brought you to the doorstep of Sundays.

There is a chance that Sundays are a day to take a breather, for at least a smidgeon of Sunday's hours, not all of Sunday since there is usually other tasks to be undertaken in this frenetic world of ours.

If the capacity of autonomous cars is such that it can meet demand on the busy weekdays, what happens to the "over-supply" that will exist on weekends and especially on Sundays, if indeed Sunday ends-up a lesser usage day?

Here's two possibilities:

1. Owners of autonomous cars which are being used for ridesharing will offer discounts on taking Sunday rides, desirous of keeping their money-making machines in-action and making money, albeit at a tightened profit margin on Sundays, and it is conceivable too that by offering such Sunday discounts it could lead to brand loyalty, getting those Sunday-going passengers to then use their particular ridesharing service during the more profitable weekday traveling.

2. Individual owners of autonomous cars might decide that rather than trying to squeeze out some extra bucks on Sundays, they will go ahead and use their autonomous car for their own interests, including undertaking a leisurely Sunday drive with the family.

I'll address the second point with some added clarifications.

Let's assume that you individually own an autonomous car that is being used for ridesharing to buck-up your income. This creates enormous pressure within your family to avoid using your ridesharing money-maker for family purposes, since doing so "robs" the cash to be made when that driverless car is used by paying customers.

Oddly enough, it means that owning an autonomous car might be akin to my situation of our family having had only one car, a limited resource. Your owning an autonomous car will require a continual balance of using it for non-paying purposes, such as your own family use, versus using it as part of a ridesharing profit-seeking venture.

When then can you potentially make use of your beloved autonomous car that you decided to purchase? Well, when it is at its lowest utility value in the marketplace, which I'm arguing would likely be on Sundays.

We then have a confluence of the family all being extraordinarily busy during the week, taking individual rides as needed in autonomous cars, either your own or someone else's, fragmenting the family unit, in a manner of speaking, and on Sundays your owned autonomous car not pressuring you as to having to quite make the dough, meaning that you and the family can go for a ride in your owned autonomous car, perhaps on those sunny Sunday afternoons.

Conclusion

That's quite a portrayal of the future involving autonomous cars.

I hope you can see the logic about why it could return us to an era of Sunday family-oriented trips for fun.

Plus, assuming that autonomous cars are likely to be EVs (which makes sense due to the electrical power needed for the AI systems and sensors), the pollution aspects are lessened in comparison to gasoline powered vehicles, so you can feel a little bit better about such superfluous driving (hey, I don't want to be a killjoy but of course the electrical power being consumed on those Sunday drives will need to come from someplace, such as hefty power plants; as such, that's a "polluter" aspect you might want to include into your calculus).

Where will you be going in your autonomous car on those Sunday drives?

Well, the Machine Learning (ML) capability of driverless cars might figure out over time the places you and your family like to visit, and you can just tell the AI self-driving car to surprise you and the family and drive to a destination that the AI suggests is a good fit for you all.

Might that also do away with those Sunday drive "heated arguments" that sometimes embroil a family about where to go? Let's hope so, it'd be a nice bonus for ensuring a serene family drive.

CHAPTER 6

FACE RECOG BANS AND AI SELF-DRIVING CARS

CHAPTER 6
FACE RECOG BANS AND AI SELF-DRIVING CAR

Recent headlines have made well-known the ban that San Francisco has enacted on facial recognition within the borders of their town, becoming the first major city to take such action, and some assert this exemplar will not be the last, even potentially opening the regulatory floodgates toward a mounting wave of similar directives.

In spite of the breathless headings, the ban is not quite what it seems on the surface. The scope is limited to the use of such technology by the city departments of San Francisco, plus there are a number of carveouts and exceptions allowed in the new regulation.

Thus, this city-bold proclamation does not encompass say federal agencies, it doesn't encompass private companies by-and-large, and it doesn't "ban" the city departments per se since it also allows for exigent circumstances for the city departments to possibly make use of facial recognition technology (meanwhile, the regulation tries to mitigate this exclusionary allowance by requiring justification and some transparency in reporting on what and why the presumed intrusive act was undertaken).

What is especially striking is that among the nationwide heated debates about the societal value of facial recognition, with strong cases being made on either side of whether to ban or not ban, in a sense the city of San Francisco has made their decision and laid down the gauntlet on the matter, namely this is what the proclamation indicates:

"The propensity for facial recognition technology to endanger civil rights and civil liberties substantially outweighs its purported benefits, and the technology will exacerbate racial injustice and threaten our ability to live free of continuous government monitoring."

Notice that there is an unequivocal calculus proclaimed that the societal costs of facial recognition outweigh the societal benefits. No confusion there.

For some, this is a weighing of the scale that does not quite fit to their assessment of the tradeoffs involved in utilizing facial recognition. There are those that would be quick to point out that when there is a widespread act producing horrific carnage, and if facial recognition could be used to find and catch the culprits, the benefits of facial recognition are well-justified as to potentially preventing further carnage and stopping the criminals cold.

In fact, perhaps surprising to some, the San Francisco regulation tends to recognize this exigency, by providing this carveout:

"Exigent circumstances means an emergency involving imminent danger of death or serious physical injury to any person that requires the immediate use of Surveillance Technology or the information it provides."

And so this exception clause would seem to allow for the prevention of facial recognition predominantly whilst also sensibly making use of it when a dire situation merits doing so.

But there's a crucial factor to be considered about this idea of being able to suddenly turn-on a switch and make use of facial recognition, namely that if the overall ban has pretty much precluded putting such technology into place, how can you all of a sudden on the spur of the moment make it magically appear and leverage it?

This would seem like a rather incredible feat of pulling a rabbit out of a hat, for which there wasn't a rabbit put into the hat to begin with (oops, sorry, spoiler alert about the rabbit in the hat magical trick). If the city departments know they aren't supposed to generally be using facial recognition, presumably they aren't going to invest in buying, deploying, and keeping it active, merely to await the day or hour that it might urgently be needed. Thus, the exception clause almost seems like a false carveout due to not being especially practical given the overall tone and demeanor of the proclamation.

Here's a question for you, would the advent of autonomous cars impact such a ban and if so in what ways?

I'm glad that you are willing to ponder the question, since I've got some thoughts about it that you might find of interest.

Autonomous Cars And Recognition Technology

For true autonomous cars, those of the Level 5 and Level 4, and to some degree the semi-autonomous cars as well at Level 2 and Level 3, there is usually a slew of sensory devices included into the car for purposes of sensing the surroundings of the car, including the use of cameras, radar units, ultrasonic devices, LIDAR, thermal detection subsystems, etc.

Cameras are pointed outward to capture the visual aspects of what is nearby to a driverless car, collecting streaming video images that are then processed by the AI on-board of the vehicle. This allows the AI to try and figure out that there is a bicyclist over there, a pedestrian up on the curb, and another car is ahead and moving at a good clip.

Vision processing is akin to the "eyes" of the self-driving car, enabling the AI to scan for objects that are stationary and are in-motion, along with classifying the objects as to what they might be and what they portend for the driverless car.

Currently, the vision processing capabilities of autonomous cars are normally only concentrating on objects as a kind of blob. For example, the human that's standing at the street corner waiting for the light to change and might cross the street, well, it is a human being that is likely an adult since their height is six feet or so, but otherwise the human is not further classified or visually dichotomized.

There's no particular reason that the visual analysis couldn't go further.

Assuming the camera is good enough to capture a high-quality image, and assuming that you've got sufficient computing capabilities packed into the driverless car, the AI system could try to do some more in-depth processing and figure out that the human being is likely a male, favoring their right leg, carrying a briefcase, and wears glasses. This is somewhat easy to visually calculate by merely inspecting the picture images being collected.

Guess what, this could also include doing facial recognition.

I'd like to have you soak in that point. I'll wait.

Why is this a point worthy of some in-depth contemplation?

Because once there is widespread use of autonomous cars, it implies that there is a possibility of having those roaming and continually roving driverless cars acting as a facial recognizer that could potentially track lots and lots of people as they proceed to walk around during their daily lives.

Think about the number of cars that go past you as you walk in any downtown city, making your way from your office to the local pub for an afterwork respite. Now, imagine that many or say even all of those cars had video recorders, plus those cars were analyzing the video in real-time and doing facial recognition.

If we could stitch together the findings of those cars, admittedly a bit of a difficulty having to get the data from those disparate cars, but possible, we could likely tell you, or anyone else, where you walked, how long it took, whether you were looking up or down or toward a billboard, whether you were happy or sad, whether you were talking and possibly even do some lip reading analysis via the on-board computer to know what you said, and so on.

Plus, since most autonomous cars are going to be electronically transmitting their on-board data up to the cloud, this data about you and the facial recognizing analysis could be done on a much larger scale, tying you to every act of being outside, such as in the morning capturing the fact that you came out of your home to get the daily newspaper on your driveway and then got into your car, and then you during work in the afternoon went outside to get your lunch, and then at the end of the workday you walked over to the pub.

I realize that some will say I am trying to suggest the sky is falling, which might seem that way, but it is simply the reality of what might be possible down-the-road, once we have a prevalence of autonomous cars on our public roadways.

All of this is technologically feasible, already, and it is more a matter of whether the automakers and tech firms would want to implement something like this, and whether society would want them to or might balk at the adoption of a seemingly intrusive form of automated recognition. As earlier mentioned, there are tradeoffs of whether this kind of Big Brother approach will make our lives worse, or whether the potential benefits would make it tenable.

Conclusion

I've so far herein focused on facial recognition, which is the presumed scope of the San Francisco ban, as per the headlines, but I think that perhaps some of the media did not go the trouble to actually read the formal regulation, which states:

"Surveillance Technology means any software, electronic device, system utilizing an electronic device, or similar device used, designed, or primarily intended to collect, retain, process, or share audio, electronic, visual, location, thermal, biometric, olfactory or similar information specifically associated with, or capable of being associated with, any individual or group."

Please carefully read and digest that statement from the regulation. It's quite a bit broader by far than merely facial recognition. In that manner, you could say that likely any or all of the sensory devices of an autonomous car would be encompassed.

Which, in view of the desire to apparently prevent tracking of us humans, the regulation appears to be trying to ensure that no loopholes are allowed. Keep in mind that the facial recognition that could be undertaken via the cameras of a driverless car could be augmented by or perhaps even directly undertaken via the other kinds of sensors on-board too. It's definitely harder to use those other sensors for quite the same reliability of tracking a person, but they could certainly help in doing so.

The final comment herein about the San Francisco ban involves this equally important point that seemed to not grab the attention of the widespread media:

"Ordinance amending the Administrative Code to require that City departments acquiring Surveillance Technology, or entering into agreements to receive information from non-City owned Surveillance Technology…"

The rub on this point is that the city departments aren't supposed to acquire (and presumably nor put in place) these technologies, something that I think was already generally expected via the ban, and nor enter into agreements to get such data from others such as private businesses. That's an intriguing extension, and I suppose once again fits with trying to tie off any loopholes.

I'll return to my rabbit in the hat point, and emphasize that suppose a firm like an automaker or tech said it could provide to the city an ability to rapidly scan across all of its fleet of driverless cars to find a mass killer that has just performed an unspeakable act. In theory, this kind of prior arrangement would be precluded, thus, making it harder to try and leverage the capability, doing so for the benefit of the city, on a spur of the moment matter.

One last thought on this is whether the emergency vehicles to be used by the city are within the scope of this ban, which it certainly seems that they are, and once those police cars, ambulances, fire trucks, and the like are either semi-autonomous or autonomous, they too would by definition have the sensory devices for collecting video and other aspects, of which, the possibility of doing facial recognition (or other kinds of recognition) would be feasible. It will be interesting to see how the city wrestles with this aspect.

All told, I'm not arguing that the societal benefits outweigh the societal costs, and nor am I claiming that the societal costs outweigh the societal benefits, but instead trying to awaken us as a society to the approaching era upon which the prevalence of self-driving driverless autonomous cars will force us to inevitably decide how to cope with pervasive technology that simultaneously opens a pandoras box and opens a cornucopia horn-of-plenty.

CHAPTER 7

STATES ON-THE-HOOK AND AI SELF-DRIVING CARS

CHAPTER 7
STATES ON-THE-HOOK AND AI SELF-DRIVING CARS

Here's a question that some politicians and regulators are silently grappling with, albeit some think that they have the unarguably "right" answer and thusly have no need to lose sleep over the matter:

Should states, counties, cities, and townships be eagerly courting self-driving driverless autonomous cars, onto their public roadways, or should those jurisdictions be neutral about inviting them into their locales, or should those governmental authorities be highly questioning and require "proof until proven safe" before the doors to their communities let even one such autonomous car onto their turf?

Part of the answer might relate to a point that I brought up during a panel at the recent AutoSens conference in Detroit, taking place last month and returning to Detroit next year on May 12-14, 2020 (plus, two international offerings, September 17-19, 2019 in Brussels and November 17-19, 2020 in Hong Kong).

The panel was focused on the regulatory landscape of self-driving cars and had the esteemed panelists of Bryant Walker Smith, University of South Carolina faculty member in the School of Law and the School of Engineering, along with Gail Gottehrer, Founder, Law Office of Gail Gottehrer LLC.

The discussion included aspects about which locales in the United States have gone out of their way to court automakers and tech firms to bring their public roadway tryouts into their jurisdictions, and which ones have not yet taken that (some would say) bold step. So far, about half of the states have some kind of legislation related to autonomous cars, but only a few have overtly sought to have autonomous cars in their realm, plus the automakers and tech firms are being choosy too about where they want to start their public efforts.

It's a kind of dual courtship, one might say.

Probably most would agree that Arizona seems to have especially rolled out the welcome mat, and those that closely follow these matters will distinctly remember the governor there that in December 2016 stated: "Arizona welcomes Uber self-driving cars with open arms and wide open roads. While California puts the brakes on innovation and change with more bureaucracy and more regulation, Arizona is paving the way for new technology and new businesses."

Sometimes the competitive juices between states or other jurisdictions can spark efforts to attract a new innovation. Good or bad, depending upon your viewpoint.

Solid Reasons To Gateway Into Driverless Cars

In the case of autonomous cars, there is a chance that the locale inviting self-driving driverless cars might get a glow of being high-tech embracers and could lead to a veritable stampede of other tech firms clamoring to come into that location.

This might mean added jobs to the region.

It might mean economic expansion as firms related to the tech opt to setup shop and make local investments.

Overall, this can make the authorities of the particular locale look smart, hip, and allow them to catch the wave on a hot innovation that will propel them and their local into the national spotlight.

A potential win-win.

Not Necessarily A Rose Garden To Embrace Public Tryouts

There is a downside though that can also sometimes bite the early adopters of new tech.

Last year, the headlines blared when an Uber self-driving car ran into and killed a pedestrian in Tempe, Arizona that was jaywalking across the street, doing so at nighttime, and the Uber self-driving car did not avoid the crash and nor did the human back-up driver avoid or even react to avert the fatal hit. It was a sad moment and has become a (hopefully) notable cautionary sign about these experimental public roadway tryouts underway.

At the time, I posted right away a preliminary analysis about what I thought might have gone awry, though based on only the sketchy details known, and it turns out that months later when the official crash report came out that I was labeled by the media as "prescient" about my prediction (which, wasn't really that much of a guess since I had been forewarning that such incidents would happen, including the autonomous car mistakes that occurred and also the dangers of relying upon human back-up drivers).

Some critics that had been otherwise unnoticed about Arizona's pursuit of autonomous car public tryouts were quick to say that the state was considered the "wild west" of self-driving car usage and the incident highlighted that there was "no sheriff in town" that ought to be closely controlling the efforts.

By the way, for clarification, note that there's a difference between locales that seek automakers and tech teams to come and do development work, pretty much a desk job kind of activity, and make use of closed track or proving grounds testing, usually apart from the public roadways, versus those locales that open their roadways to self-driving cars as a type of grand experiment for those that live, drive, work, bike, and walk there.

This puts the citizenry at some danger if a driverless car goes awry, and as already indicated, having a human back-up driver is no guarantee that incidents will always be circumvented.

I've also been waiting to see a potential backlash on the possibility of the jobs lost side of the ledger, for a particular jurisdiction, namely that if indeed autonomous cars become prevalent there, some worry there will be a lose of driving-related jobs, including ridesharing drivers, cab drivers, limo drivers, delivery drivers, and the like would take a heavy economic toll. I do though quickly point out that we are a long ways from that kind of future, since it would require widespread adoption of driverless cars, which we are not even close to yet achieving.

Are Locales Responsible When Mishaps Or Crashes Occur

Now that I've brought you somewhat up-to-speed on the topic of the tradeoff for locales about whether to consider embracing driverless car tryouts or perhaps remaining neutral about them or possibly erecting barriers until satisfied that it is time to let such cars in, let's get to my related question that can be another humongous factor.

Would a jurisdiction be on-the-hook if an autonomous car mishap or crash occurs within their boundaries?

What especially prompted me to bring up the question at the AutoSens panel was that the Uber incident has gotten a new twist recently when family members of the killed pedestrian launched a $10 million claim against the city of Tempe, asserting that the city had some responsibility in the matter.

You might at first glance be bewildered as to why the city might hold any responsibility. We would all likely assume that Uber would be the mainstay of attention to the matter, since it was their car, their human back-up driver, and otherwise their efforts that contributed to the deadly crash.

In this case, it turns out that the median area from which the pedestrian wandered into the street as a jaywalker had been previously setup as a brick pathway that appears to lead you to a curb point that is not at a crosswalk. Therefore, one might argue that it was an invitation to jaywalk and could be confusing for any pedestrian that might find themselves at that juncture. The filed claim also points out that the city subsequently removed the walkway and put rocks and plants in there instead.

I'm not going to get mired herein in the aspect about the pathway (it will be interesting to see how it plays out in court), since it tangentially is related to my primary theme of this discussion.

Let's return instead to the overarching question about the responsibility that a jurisdiction might bear for having invited into their midst the vaunted autonomous car public roadway tryouts.

Here's some considerations:

- Did the jurisdiction sufficiently vet the inclusion of autonomous cars and take "warranted" steps to ensure the safety of pedestrians and other drivers regarding the public roadway tryouts?

- Did the jurisdiction put in place ongoing efforts to monitor and track the autonomous car public roadway tryouts, doing so to keep ahead of potential mishaps or crashes?

- Did the jurisdiction establish any requirements or constraints about where, when, and other facets of the allowed public roadway tryouts, taking into account the existing infrastructure and populous in their jurisdiction?

- Did the jurisdiction take a rush-to-judgment about allowing public roadway tryouts and fail to perform its sovereign duties in protecting those within its boundaries?

For a handy legal analysis on such topics, consider taking a look at a paper sponsored by the Transportation Research Board (TRB) and their National Cooperative Highway Research Program (NCHRP) as written by authors at the Santa Clara University School of Law, which is a useful starting point to learn more about these matters.

Conclusion

Some would argue that a jurisdiction should have at top-of-mind the safety of their populous, and that in a haste to welcome new innovations they can circumvent the normal rigors that should be observed.

Others say that any jurisdiction that wants to stick with the usual bureaucratic rigors will likely be the last to gain the benefits of new innovations.

It can be a tough choice.

Of course, there are numerous legal protections for jurisdictions such as potential sovereign immunity and statutory limits to what their monetary and other liability might be. Is there a duty of care that might be breeched by allowing driverless car public roadway tryouts? Is a laissez faire approach suitable, or should a more heavy-handed line be used?

This has not yet stood the test of the courts, and nor the court of public opinion.

For politicians and regulators, these initial driverless car tryouts can be a boon or a bust, and though some might think they know the answer to saying avidly yes, or being neutral, or saying to go more cautiously, only time will tell which of those options turned out to be most prudent.

CHAPTER 8
SENSORS PROFITING AND AI SELF-DRIVING CARS

CHAPTER 8
SENSORS PROFITING AND AI SELF-DRIVING CARS

At many of my speaking engagements on self-driving driverless autonomous cars, beyond the usual technology-based questions, I also oftentimes get asked various business-oriented questions about whether or not autonomous cars will be profitable.

You might have already assumed that self-driving cars will be profit making vehicles.

Indeed, it is certainly a natural assumption to make. Why in the world would all of these automakers and tech firms be toiling away at trying to make, build, test, and deploy driverless cars unless they felt pretty strongly that there was a decent profit to be made.

In fact, some are suggesting that whomever gets to the vaunted true autonomous car first, the Level 5 which will have an on-board AI system driver that can take you anyplace that a human driver could, will be in the bucks, they'll get the reward of vast riches for their labors, and be soaking in obscene amounts of money.

Some AI developers are slogging forward because the Level 5 is a moonshot-like challenge and offers a puzzle to be solved unlike any they might otherwise encounter (in some respects, the challenge being more important to them than the money aspects per se). Some are interested in the acclaim from being able to fully execute the "mother of all AI projects" as proclaimed by Apple CEO Tim Cook. Some hope that achieving an autonomous car will democratize mobility, freeing people to get around, and revolutionize how our society functions.

Some want the money, or possibly a combination of the aforementioned loftier aspirations plus the money.

Ways We Make Money From Cars

The most obvious ways that everyone imagines that there is profit to be had will be these traditional kinds of modes:

- Selling autonomous cars
- Renting out autonomous cars
- Delivering via autonomous cars
- Ridesharing out autonomous cars

If you ponder those key modes, it really doesn't seem to be much different than today's world and contemporary conventional cars.

You can make a profit by selling conventional cars.

You can make a profit by renting out conventional cars, though admittedly the car rental agencies are a bit queasy about a future of driverless cars and how that will mess with the renting of cars.

There's also the use of cars to do deliveries, such as the current craze of getting a taco and burrito delivered to your door at midnight, which many are already experimenting with via using autonomous vehicles lesser than full-on cars to do this kind of simpler and more bounded act.

You can maybe make money by ridesharing out conventional cars, but the record so far of Uber and Lyft doesn't give you any warm and fuzzies that a real profit is to be readily had (they are losing money hand-over-fist, though some say this is just the early part of the service life cycle when trying to grab market share and gain a loyal base, so you need to expect that sometimes you have to spend money to ultimately later on make money).

For ridesharing of conventional cars, the difficulty of trying to eek out a profit involves all of the costs associated with the ridesharing arrangements. Pundits are expecting that once the human driver of the ridesharing car is excised from the deal, which presumably will take place once autonomous cars are safe and available, the most significant cost that has been a presumed major impediment toward profitability will be off-the0table (i.e., human driver labor).

Smooth sailing afterward, they assume. The thing is that we don't really know yet what the financial numbers will really look like. What will be the cost of the AI system and its ongoing updates and maintenance? Will there need to be special kind of insurance for driverless cars and how costly will it be? And so on.

Let's though put aside the usual modes of making money from a car, whether it be autonomous or not, and use our thinking caps to find other ways to make money from a car.

Other Ways To Make Money From Cars

I'll give you a clue about another likely significant way to make money via a car, especially down-the-road in an era of driverless cars (that's a teaser, a spoiler alert of what I'm about to reveal!).

Recently, ridesharing drivers have been selling their eyeballs, well, the use of their eyeballs, by contracting with real estate firms that are trying to find houses to flip.

If you are an Uber or Lyft driver, you are presumably roving around for hours on end, hopefully with paying passengers on-board, most of the time, and have not much else to do other than drive the car. I realize that human drivers are supposed to be fully attentive to the roadway and traffic, but I think we all know that humans aren't nearly that singularly focused when behind the wheel.

So, a ridesharing driver can easily keep their eyes peeled for any houses that seem to be viable house flippers.

Usually, telltale signs are when a house looks like it is pretty much semi-abandoned, including that the front lawn is disheveled, there might be posted signs warning that the property is in violation of homeowner's ordinances, and so on. It's pretty easy for a ridesharing driver to be watchful for such houses. Once they spot a potential house flipping candidate, they either write down what they spotted, or enter it into a mobile app, and they've just completed a tidy extra task.

Along with the tidy extra task comes the potential for getting a tidy fee from the real estate firm seeking houses to be flipped.

In short, another way to make money and possibly profit from a car would be to use the car as a handy platform from which to traverse an area and find or detect something that others would be willing to pay to know about.

Fortunately, autonomous cars are going to be able to do this in spades, escalating exponentially the capability to rove and scan, it's in their bloodline, one might say.

Driverless Cars As Roving Golden Eyeballs

Imagine that there are autonomous cars undertaking ridesharing.

Some assert that this is going to be a springboard towards ridesharing on a volume and scale that we can hardly conceive of. If that's the case, there are going to be driverless cars roaming and roving all over the place, taking human passengers to their destinations, picking up human passengers that need a ride, and otherwise trying to be in the right places at the right times.

For purposes of being a driverless car, the vehicle is jam packed with sensors. The sensors include multiple cameras, collecting visual video and images that are being interpreted by the AI to figure out where the road is, where to turn, whether pedestrians are nearby, etc. Plus, there are other sensors including likely radar, ultrasonic units, LIDAR, thermal devices, audio listening devices, and a cornucopia of similar sensors.

The mainstay at first will be that those sensors are there for the purpose of driving the car. Don't mess with the sensors or the on-board computer processors for anything besides making sure the autonomous car can safely get from point A to point B. I'm betting that there will be some extra computational cycles available, perhaps normally kept in reserve for situations of a tight or tough driving situation, and yet otherwise could be used for other aspects, if needed, when viable to leverage.

Why not have the AI look for houses to be flipped?

It would be relatively easy to do.

The data pouring in from the cameras is already going to be undergoing analyses. You could either have the vision processing system tag the images of houses and in real-time be marking ones that could be house flippers, or, you could set aside for the moment the house flipper search and have that undertaken in more idle moments.

For driverless cars, there will be idle moments for example when sitting at a red light. You and I likely daydream when at a red light, but the computer processers on-board can be doing some real work, like rescanning images to find those house flippers.

Or, maybe when the driverless car is getting charged-up at an EV charging station (most self-driving cars are likely to be EV's), during that idle time the processors can be doing constructive acts such as filtering the collected data for houses meeting the house flipping criteria.

Let's kick this up a notch.

Fleets of driverless cars will be likely uploading their individually collected data to the cloud database of the automaker or tech firm (or other). The uploaded data might already have been examined for houses to be flipped, or this might be a task undertaken once the data has been pushed up into the cloud (sparing the on-board AI systems this task).

The collective "wisdom" of hundreds or say thousands of driverless cars that have been whisking around towns and cities, well, it's a treasure trove of handy data.

What Will The Eyed Data Be Used For

Think about the possibilities.

You are a local house painter and you are trying to find out which homes in the county need a paint job.

Easy, just consult a database of houses that have been "seen" by a fleet of driverless cars.

You can search the database by where the house is, when it was most recently seen, and pull-up an image or two (or a video) that shows what it looks like. The AI can already pre-assess which homes have faded or peeling paint, so you don't need to cull the list.

This can be tied to another database of homeowner records, and with the touch of a button you can be on the phone to the homeowner, explaining how wonderful their house would look if painted in green.

You can even text them a photoshopped version of their house with the color changed.

Right now, we often take a look at a large database such as the one maintained by Google, trying to see what a house looks like. Those images are often dated, and there are only so many times that they are able to send out their handful of photo-taking cars to capture an area. With driverless cars, assuming they are already on a ridesharing quest, this photo-taking or video-taking is part-and-parcel of what they are already doing. No added cost, in a manner of speaking.

It is conceivable that via various ways to make money from the driverless car collected data, it might motivate the autonomous car owner to keep their self-driving car on-the-go, even when there aren't any paying passengers needing a ride.

If the money is good enough, it might be better to actually avoid taking rides, since those passengers expect to get to their desired destination, which might not be where your driverless car needs to go to collect money-making data.

Downsides Of the Madcap Data Collecting

The world is never accommodating to having only benefits and no costs, or so it seems.

In the case of the driverless car data collection, once a particular neighborhood has been scanned, the question arises about what good does it do to potentially scan it again a few hours later. In essence, it could be that the data won't have quite the payoff at all times as might be hoped for.

Plus, if one fleet has already done that neighborhood, and a different fleet does so, this will rachet up competition in terms of these collected databases, meaning that there might not be as much profit as one would have if only one fleet had the golden goose and no others did.

The privacy implications of this kind of vast and unending data collection can be quite staggering when you sit down and think about it. I've only mentioned the notion of scanning to find houses, but it is perhaps obvious that the scanning of the images can look for many more objects, including human beings in the images.

Want to know where your significant other was yesterday? Log into a cloud database of a fleet of driverless cars, give it a picture of your partner, and let it find them, reporting to you that the person was seen in front of the pancake restaurant, then later on seen at the local park, then at the door of an apartment in downtown, and so on.

Conclusion

The main theme of this discussion was to consider ways to make money from autonomous cars, beyond the obvious means that we do today with conventional cars. A key difference of conventional cars and driverless cars is that you'll have a full suite of sensors, collecting data wherever the self-driving car goes, and the data can be kept and analyzed on-board the driverless car or placed into the cloud and used there.

This can be done in a scale and in a manner not feasible for what human drivers could do. There are likely money-making ways to leverage this that no one has yet envisioned and will emerge once self-driving cars become prevalent. Try to figure that out, before everyone else does.

CHAPTER 9
UNRULY DRIVERS
AND
AI SELF-DRIVING CARS

CHAPTER 9
UNRULY RIDERS AND AI SELF-DRIVING CARS

I'm sure that we've all had occasions to rate our ridesharing drivers, typically on a scale of 1 (worst) to 5 (best), but did you also know that many ridesharing drivers are able to rate you too, the passenger in their ridesharing car?

When the rating of passengers by ridesharing drivers was initially proclaimed in the media, there was a backlash by some that felt this was the shoe being put on the wrong foot. A passenger is the customer, therefore rightfully as a client should be able to render judgment about their service provider (i.e., the ridesharing driver) and opt to do so when they wish and with whatever rating they want to assign, but it seemed quite untoward to let the driver rate the passenger.

Some felt that this put too much of an onus on the passenger, meaning that apparently you would have to bring cookies and flowers to your driver, you would need to listen when the driver drones endlessly about their day, and you'd have to give a hearty thanks and a pat on the back upon ending the ride, lest you might get dinged in the ratings.

Intolerable. Unfathomable. Just plain wrongheaded.

Other than the psychological "damages" of getting a low rating as a passenger, it was pointed out that the ridesharing services didn't particularly use the passenger ratings per se.

Sure, an astute ridesharing driver that is being summoned by a passenger could take a peak at the rating of that potential rider, and maybe decide to gird themselves for a tough and tortuous ride, possibly even electronically dumping the candidate rider with some excuse like the driver can't get there in time, yet it was a pretty unlikely that there were any serious consequences as a penalty for sour-rated passengers.

It appears the ante is being upped by a recent indication that Uber says it will start banning riders that have "significantly below average" ratings. That's right, you might get yourself into the ridesharing doghouse and be banned from even being able to seek out rides on the ridesharing network once you've been blacklisted.

Once again, there has been some consternation voiced that this kind of ban is not right, and the rider ratings game is getting out-of-hand.

Problems Associated With Ratings Of Riders

Suppose a passenger has unfairly gotten dinged by drivers and ended-up with a lesser rating accordingly. Some wonder, suspiciously, might the lower rating be due to something other than a bona fide reason?

Bona fide reasons are presumably things like getting into a ridesharing car and ripping up the upholstery, which is a costly untoward act, given that the drivers usually own their car, their key source of income for ridesharing, and then they have to get repairs made. Plus, the driver is potentially losing money by not taking fares while getting the repairs done. Or, the driver opts to continue driving with the torn seat, which them gets them dinged ratings-wise by passengers for having an unkept car (thus, lowering the driver's rating and endangering their livelihood).

A more terrifying reason that drivers might give out a lowered rating to a passenger involves situations whereby the rider threatens the driver. Maybe the rider is a nutty person and prone to violence. Maybe the passenger is a sane person but has had a rotten day and decides to take it out on the driver. Maybe the passenger was triggered by a comment that the driver made, such as when sometimes a driver misguidedly starts to discus politics, and it gets the passenger riled up since they hold a completely diametric view on the topic.

Those that are worried about the passenger ratings are quick to point out that a driver might intentionally assign a lowered score to a passenger for the wrong reasons, perhaps because the driver didn't like how the person looked or the clothing they were wearing. Perhaps a passenger got a lower rating because of their political positions, exhibited by what they said to the driver or maybe wearing a button or badge that indicates their political preference.

The passenger ratings might be an amalgamation of discrimination and bigotry, hiding as a seemingly unbiased numeric score for which there would seem to be no ready way to unwrap how it came to be.

Here's an interesting question to ponder, namely, what might occur with the advent of self-driving driverless autonomous cars as it pertains to the controversial notion about ratings of riders?

Next Up Is Ratings Of Riders While In Autonomous Cars

There are pundits that suggest there will never be any rider ratings anymore once we are past the era of human drivers at the ridesharing wheel and are fully immersed in an era of autonomous cars. Thus, presumably, assuming that those biased or knee-jerk ratings by human drivers are no longer going to occur, there's no chance of any kind of foul ratings that embed intolerable biases.

I'd say that those pundits are only half-right, at best.

Ratings of ridesharing passengers are undoubtably going to continue. In fact, the rider ratings will take on an even greater role than they do today. It is going to be unstoppable.

Yikes, how can that be?

Let's consider the reasons for this.

A human ridesharing driver does more than simply drive a car. In a sense, the human driver is also the civility cop in the vehicle. In theory, the driver wants a passenger to remain calm and not bash or tear-up the car. The driver would also be likely to try and suppress or limit antics such as a passenger that rolls down the car window and yells obscenities at pedestrians on the sidewalk.

In short, generally, the human driver is a kind of human watchkeeper that by their very presence tends to keep passengers from, frankly, going berserk.

A passenger doesn't even necessarily need to be told to be civil, since they know overall that the human driver is a witness to any untoward acts and might either directly try to stop something troublesome or report it to other authorities.

I realize that some of you might right away be complaining that it is nonsense to suggest that ridesharing drivers are the perfection of politeness and civility. Don't put words into my mouth, thanks. I am not saying they are. Instead, I am merely pointing out that as maybe as foulmouthed that a driver might be, they are going to usually be suppressing any way-out-there antics of a passenger (I am also not saying that all passengers are unruly, you need to though acknowledge that some are or can become so).

Shift your gaze into the future when there are self-driving driverless cars whizzing around our streets, highways, and byways. For true Level 5 autonomous cars, there isn't a human driver in the car. The car will either have passengers or might be empty.

By definition, an empty autonomous car does not have any need to rate a passenger, since there's isn't a passenger present.

Would it be useful to rate the passengers in an autonomous car?

Yes, of course.

Ways To Deal With Unruly Riders In Self-Driving Cars

Without a human driver in the self-driving car, you've seemingly removed the last line of defense toward catching and suppressing ill-advised human behavior of the passengers. A rider in a self-driving car might decide it's a great place to mark graffiti, easier and more likely to be seen than trying to do the same on a back-roads billboard or tree covered street sign.

Passengers in a driverless car might decide it is a good time to have a paintball fight. Or, roll down the windows and shoot paintballs at other cars and innocents walking down the street.

As they say, people do the darnedest things.

Especially when they think they aren't being watched, won't be detected, and won't be caught or have to atone for their actions. If this seems like a sad comment about humanity, sorry, it just seems to be the case for some, though thankfully perhaps not all of us.

How To Do Ratings Of Riders In Autonomous Cars

I assume that you are now of the mind that maybe it does make sense to try and limit how much emblazoned craziness that passengers in autonomous cars might try to undertake.

Here's the likely solutions:

- Inward pointing cameras will allow the video recording of passengers, similar to how stores mount cameras and warn that you might be caught shoplifting, doing so to warn everyone, even though only a small fraction of patrons is presumably going to do some thievery.

- The AI system can use the camera video to do a real-time analysis and possibly detect in-the-moment when passengers tip over into being unruly, and immediately machine-voice a concern to the passenger, which might then prevent unruliness right away (versus merely video recording as a means of post-damage evidence).

- Using sophisticated Natural Language Processing (NLP), the AI might do more than just a perfunctory robotic-like warning, and carry on a dialogue with the passengers, explaining in a more fluent manner what they are doing wrong and why they should stop doing so. Note, I've spoken and written about this kind of NLP, along with cautioning that it might be anthropomorphized beyond sensibility.

- If needed, the AI system could potentially ring-up a remote human operator, similar to an OnStar-like service, and notify the operator that there's something afoul occurring, allowing the operator to then directly interact with the passengers, possibly further convincing the riders to cease-and-desist (the "operator" doesn't necessarily have access to the driving controls, they are more so for reaching a human to offer human-like reasoning and assistance, remotely).

- In a perhaps worst-case scenario, the AI could contact 911 and report what's going on, or in a perhaps scarier act change where the self-driving car is going and route to the nearest police or other authority.

- All or a combination of those aforementioned aspects are real possibilities.

It would behoove the owner of the self-driving car to maintain a rating of passengers.

This would allow the autonomous car to either know what to expect from a potential rider, or for the ridesharing network to algorithmically opt to refuse to send a self-driving car to the requester.

And, a rider rating serves as an additional "be notified" kind of signal or warning to prospective passengers, allowing riders to realize beforehand that their actions inside an autonomous car will have various potential ramifications. Otherwise, a rider could just keep riding in driverless cars and beat them all up, staying low enough in their untoward acts that they might get a real-time rebuke and nothing more.

Maybe, some suggest, there might be specially outfitted self-driving cars that are hardened internally to accommodate those wild passengers (like padded cells, perhaps, some sardonically say).

Others say that autonomous cars should as a minimum not allow the windows to be rolled down, preventing any antics involving tossing things out the window or voicing outward insults, but this seems like a doubtful approach and it is unlikely the ridesharing public would sacrifice the window roll-down as a result of the oft chance of others misbehaving (I suppose the ability to roll-down a window could be based on your passenger rating).

Conclusion

Overall, the reviled rider rating is not going to disappear after autonomous cars become prevalent. Such ratings will still will have merit. The owners of self-driving cars, whether fleet owners or individual owners, will want to protect their investments and will likely grab onto any viable means that will keep their driverless cars primed and ready as money making machines.

There are some added concerns underlying this matter too.

Privacy about the video recordings and AI analyses of your behavior inside a self-driving car is quite another element though that this "solution" raises, stirringly so.

Suppose you opt to take a ridesharing driverless car home after a night of fun at the local bars, and while inside the autonomous car you make a drunken spectacle. Presumably, the video and the AI caught it all. Plus, the self-driving car is likely to push this data up to the cloud database of the automaker or tech firm. Your most embarrassing moments might live forever in a database that you have no means to control.

Another concern is whether the algorithmic approach used to derive the rider rating will be truly unbiased, which doesn't necessarily need to be the case, and could instead have hidden or other capacities that embed discriminatory mathematical elements.

For readers interested further in privacy issues and also the need for algorithmic transparency as a significant societal matter that will embroil the emergence of autonomous cars, I've been covering such aspects in my writings and speeches. There is a wave coming, mark my words, and we are right now standing on the beach with a chance to do something before the water crests.

In any case, if you were hoping that rider ratings are on their way out due to the self-driving car tryouts and potential eagerness for driverless car adoption, no dice, sorry to say.

CHAPTER 10

FATHER'S DAY AND AI SELF-DRIVING CARS

CHAPTER 10
FATHER'S DAY AND AI SELF-DRIVING CARS

As readers know, I tend to be relatively serious about the topic of self-driving cars, but have opted to make an exception for this Father's Day by providing a bit more of a light-hearted "analysis" about how you could potentially use self-driving driverless autonomous cars for making Father's Day a special day for your dad.

Suppose we did really have an abundance of self-driving cars on our public roadways, what could you do to celebrate Father's Day?

Here's my Top 5 ways you could do so:

1. Have an autonomous car go pick-up your father and whisk him to a secret destination where you and others are waiting to surprise him with a Father's Day celebration. In this case, the AI driving the autonomous car would need to remain mum and not spill the beans about where he is being taken and what awaits him. Note to the AI developers at the automakers and tech firms, please add this "no tattle telling" option into your driverless car AI systems, thanks.

2. You get into a driverless car, deck-it-out on the inside, and go pick-up your father to take him on a touching journey around the neighborhood that he grew-up in, tracing his roots, and as a bonus, a really big bonus, you listen patiently to his (once again) endless stories about his childhood and act like you've never heard the stories before. You might need to turn-off the AI's vocalization since it could potentially complain about already having heard those stories and ruin the mood in the autonomous car, or worse still, finish telling each story before your father can do so (that's what Machine Learning or Deep Learning can do, so be watchful).

3. On Father's Day, you get a fleet of self-driving cars to be temporarily programmed to laugh at his dad jokes, no matter which autonomous car he happens to get into, leading him to become convinced that his sense of humor and joke telling is universally welcomed and acclaimed. Admittedly, the downside with this approach is that you'll need to gird yourself for even more such dad jokes from him thereafter. Just make sure that AI system doesn't pattern match to the jokes and decide to start telling them on its own, else none of us will ever be safe-and-sound in an autonomous car again.

4. Some fathers relish a quiet day of no duties, no ruckus, and so you arrange to have a self-driving car pick him up and take him essentially nowhere in particular, but meanwhile the inside of the driverless car, which has wall-to-wall LED screens that are usually being used to entertain while inside an autonomous car or allow for remote working efforts while commuting, those screens are filled with scenic pictures and videos of serene forests and pleasant beaches. You also intercut pics of you and the family on vacations and at the end of the no-journey journey the screens fill with you all of you in real-time live-mode wishing him a Happy Father's Day and thanking him for his tireless efforts. That will work fine if 5G is around by then.

5. Here's the topmost way -- buy him his own self-driving driverless car, and though he has always wanted a flying jet pack (he's carped about it, many times), this is the next best thing. He'll learn to love it and you certainly won't ever hear him complain about having to give you a lift to school or the mall or to piano lessons, since he'll just dispatch his own obedient autonomous car to do those fatherly errands for him.

Conclusion

Hope you liked my handy list.

Say, I'd like to thank my kids for celebrating Father's Day with me and wish all of you a wonderful and joyous day.

CHAPTER 11

SUMMONS FEATURE AND AI SELF-DRIVING CARS

CHAPTER 11
SUMMONS FEATURE
AND
AI SELF-DRIVING CARS

At a recent Tesla shareholders meeting, one topic that arose involved the newest Autopilot "Enhanced" Summon feature that is being developed and which has been made available in a beta version for some Tesla owners that are in the Tesla Early Access program.

Usually referred to as either Enhanced Summon or sometimes as Advanced Summon, the concept is that it is "a parking assist feature that helps you bring your car towards you or towards the destination of your choice by navigating out of parking spaces and maneuvering around objects as necessary" (per the reported beta release notes).

There is already an existing Summon feature available that is not considered advanced or enhanced, some say it is "classic" or "simple" Summon, while others point out it is minimally any kind of "summoning" since it involves a human using an app that directs the car to go forward or in reverse and then the vehicle attempts to proceed a short distance, such as backing out of your garage, though Tesla cautions that the car might "not detect certain obstacles, including those that are very narrow (e.g., bikes)" and thus the human remote operator is to "remain prepared to stop the vehicle at any time."

There is an ongoing argument about whether the word "Summon" aptly captures or misstates the existing simpler version, just as some also argue that the word "Autopilot" perhaps overstates the capabilities of the automation currently available on Tesla cars (suggesting that the automation can fully operate the car without human assistance, which it cannot yet do).

When asked about having missed the promised rollout date for the newer and more full-bodied Enhanced Summon feature, Elon Musk indicated that "there's a lot of complexity in parking lots, it turns out."

AI Driving Is Hard To Achieve

Some pundits were quick to point out that Musk's comment about complexity in parking lots illustrated a prevailing theme of not beforehand realizing or acknowledging how difficult it is to develop a true autonomous car capability, akin to a Level 4 or Level 5, versus a Level 2 or Level 3 set of capabilities which are semi-autonomous as is the current Tesla's.

For Level 2 and Level 3, a human licensed driver is supposed to be co-sharing the driving task with the semi-autonomous automation, versus a true full automation of Level 4 or Level 5 which is able to perform the driving task entirely without any human intervention. In theory, it is easier to develop semi-autonomous features since you can always toss the driving effort onto the shoulders of a human driver, presumably overcoming any gaps or lacking capabilities of the automation by relying upon the human driver.

Some critics worry that time and again there are misleading expectations being conveyed to the public that imply or at times assert that developing an AI system that can fully drive a car is straightforward, but this tends to misjudge and underplay the full depth and enormity of what humans do when undertaking the driving task and how complex any real-world driving environment can be.

Even in parking lots, it turns out.

In some sense of relief of not perhaps jumping the gun on releasing the Enhanced Summon on a widespread basis before it is properly ready and vetted, Musk indicated that "we don't want to like, run someone over."

He also acknowledged that in terms of sticking to predicted release dates that he is "sometimes a little optimistic about timeframes." This remark regarding stated deadlines got a bit of a chuckle when he also accompanied it with the comment that "it's time you knew" that he is perhaps optimistic (occasionally) on such matters.

Difficult Facets About Summoning A Car

You might be wondering why it is indeed apparently hard to have a car drive to you as a kind of summoning, which I might add also includes the converse act of telling your car to go find a parking spot once you've disembarked from the vehicle.

Thus, there are really two core actions:

- One action in which you have gotten out of your car at the front of a store or restaurant and you want your car to go find a place to park (a type of "dismissing" or "dispatching" of the vehicle).

- The other action is when you have come out of the store or restaurant and you want your car to pull out of its parking spot and come pick you up (a "summoning" or "hailing" of the car).

Human drivers generally seem to be able to undertake these two core actions, usually without adverse encounters, though certainly there are fender benders and at times pedestrians that get struck during these maneuvers. Normally, the parking lot traversal is at low enough speeds, and the human driver is overall attentive to the driving task, such that incidents only tend to involve minor injuries and modest property damage, rather than severe damages and actual deaths.

There are lots of objects and obstacles in most parking lots.

You've got cars that are parked in the parking lot, you've got cars that are in-motion throughout the parking lot, you've got pedestrians walking to their cars or merely crossing through the parking lot, you've got adults, you've got children, you might have animals like a dog on a leash or one that has gotten off its leash, you might have skateboarder, bicyclists, motorcyclists, people on scooters. And so on. It can be as busy as any city street.

When I helped my children learn to drive, we drove in a mall parking lot early in the morning before the mall opened, and so there were very few cars parked there, and almost no pedestrians or other moving objects. It was relatively easy for them to learn to drive at first, but when we came back to try while the mall was busy, the complexity of the environment and the hard choices of how to drive were a far cry from an empty parking lot.

Considerations About Summoning

To-date, the Autopilot Enhanced Summoning involves a human that presumably gets out of the car, and while standing outside of the car will use a mobile app to invoke the feature, doing so to either summon the vehicle or to dismiss it to park itself.

Here's some questions or thoughts to be considered:

- Is the human doing the summoning able to see with full line-of-sight the actions of the car?

The answer is potentially not.

Though the manual states that the human ought to be in line-of-sight, this allows discretion to the human, which though yes you can say that the human is ultimately responsible, but this belies the aspect that there is no system enforcement of a line-of-sight requirement and thus the human might not be aware of some untoward act that is about to occur and therefore not going to stop the car by using the mobile app accordingly.

- Is the feature restricted to solely being used in parking lots?

The answer is apparently not, as exemplified by some videos posted on the web showing some using the beta version that have their car come to then while standing down-the-street from their garage. In that sense, this feature can presumably be used in your neighborhood, essentially allowing a seemingly driverless car to be on your street. Some say that the final version might have a geo-fencing that restricts the usage to parking lots, but this is somewhat doubtful as to how the system would realize the distinction between a parking lot versus not being in a parking lot.

- Does the distance limit ensure that this will be safely used?

Currently, the stated distance limit is 150 feet, meaning that in theory you the human standing outside the car must be within 150 feet to invoke the feature. Though 150 feet might seem like a short distance, when you consider the dynamics of a busy parking lot, I think you'd agree that a lot of untoward things can happen within even just 150 feet of where you are standing. Also, some suggest that you might be able to trick the car with some electronic hacking such that you could be much further away than 150 feet, but the car doesn't realize it.

- How will this impact parking lots?

If all of us drove autonomous cars, presumably the traffic in parking lots would be improved by all of us summoning our driverless cars, which would likely also use V2V (vehicle-to-vehicle) electronic communications to coordinate their actions. We aren't yet anywhere near that day. Thus, the odds are that there will be a lot of human driven cars trying to get around a parking lot and inserted into this mix will be an occasional semi-autonomous summoned car, which given that it is not at all equivalent to a human driver would suggest that it will likely gum up the flow and create difficulties. Other than the spectate of seeing it happen, the first time, human drivers are bound to get upset with the summoning occurring in their midst.

- Is this summoning a legal capability?

It is muddled as to whether this kind of parking lot summon feature is legal or illegal. Essentially, you have a semi-autonomous vehicle that is supposed to have a driver inside attending to the co-sharing of the driving task, and instead you now have a human outside of the vehicle that is trying to remotely control some aspects of the vehicle, though they might or might not have complete access to the driving controls. Also, suppose someone hands their smartphone to their kids and tells them to go ahead and summon the car, in which case you've now got unlicensed drivers and that are not even adults, presumably acting as some form of remote driver operator. Not good.

Conclusion

I realize that some would argue that the summoning is only supposed to be used by responsible adults that are licensed to drive a car, but you are not taking into account human behavior. People don't do things that they are necessarily told they are supposed to do. This idea that you can swipe away any unsafe practices by merely pinning it to the responsibility of the human driver is really just allowing for the possibility of unchecked unsafe efforts.

In one sense, some would say that the beta program has already let the genie out of the bottle, since those Tesla owners that have access to the Enhanced Summon can already use it, as they wish, where they wish, when they wish to do so. If the feature does cross-the-line into being illegal, it would seem that the line has already been crossed, though it has not gotten any fanfare and so far has fortunately not apparently produced any publicized untoward results.

Overall, there is no question that having a robust summoning feature is something that will be a boon to the advent of self-driving driverless autonomous cars, especially since it provides an added benefit for those that might be mobility marginalized, but such a feature should only be in our real-world environment once it has proven itself to be safe and sound.

CHAPTER 12
LIBRA CRYPTOCURRENCY AND AI SELF-DRIVING CARS

CHAPTER 12
LIBRA CRYPTOCURRENCY AND AI SELF-DRIVING CARS

Yesterday, Facebook released its official white paper describing their newly being formulated cryptocurrency, called Libra, akin in some ways to what you might think of when you hear about bitcoins, essentially leveraging the use of blockchain and offering a global currency untied to any specific country, and will be guided by a non-profit entity known as the Libra Association (based in Geneva, Switzerland).

The founding members of the Libra Association offers a rather impressive set of organizations, showcasing that perhaps this won't just be a Facebook-only initiative, which is how Facebook is pitching the endeavor, namely that Facebook is at the forefront for the moment, via their regulated subsidiary Calibra, and yet they assert that they will revert to a membership role rather than a leadership role, coming in the first half of 2020 when the cryptocurrency launches.

Here's the initial set of founding members, and it is stated that a total of about 100 members is being anticipated by the formal launch:

- Payments: Mastercard, PayPal, PayU (Naspers' fintech arm), Stripe, Visa

- Technology and marketplaces: Booking Holdings, eBay, Facebook/Calibra, Farfetch, Lyft, Mercado Pago, Spotify AB, Uber Technologies, Inc.

- Telecommunications: Iliad, Vodafone Group

- Blockchain: Anchorage, Bison Trails, Coinbase, Inc., Xapo Holdings Limited

- Venture Capital: Andreessen Horowitz, Breakthrough Initiatives, Ribbit Capital, Thrive Capital, Union Square Ventures

- Nonprofit and multilateral organizations, and academic institutions: Creative Destruction Lab, Kiva, Mercy Corps, Women's World Banking

Going whole-hog into the let-freedom-ring blockchain perspective (perhaps better worded as Distributed Ledger Technology or DLT), the white paper declares that Libra will be based on open source code (rather than being proprietary programs that only Facebook could see or change), its underlying Libra network will be open to everyone, it will allow and encourage that others build additional software and services on top of the Libra framework (these other add-ons will be part of the Libra ecosystem), and overall that they hope it spurs the stated goal of "building more inclusive financial options for the world."

Some Salient Points About Libra

Obviously, this new entrant into the cryptocurrency realm will live-or-die based on its ability to be secure, otherwise few will be willing to use it for their funds and their financial data. Indeed, the white paper indicates that their basis for deciding to build something from scratch rather than using an already existent cryptocurrency is threefold:

(1) Need for scalability to accommodate an envisioned billions upon billions of accounts (once it takes hold), fast transaction processing (an often times complaint about other entrants as to being too slow), low latency (people won't be willing to wait if their monetary transaction has delays in processing), and an efficient and high-capacity storage mechanism (imagine how large the dataset will grow over time, logging billions upon billions of accounts and billions upon billions of transactions).

(2) Highly secure (something that many will likely take a wait-and-see attitude, since we've already witnessed other entrants that have had hacks and other break-in's and digital coinage thievery happen).

(3) Flexible to adjust over time and meet the needs of expanding financial services.

Some already in the realm of cryptocurrency are a bit chagrined to have it suggested that Facebook and the other founding members couldn't have chosen an already existent cryptocurrency, and are perhaps ticked-off about getting a back-handed swipe by the suggestion that nothing else could handle this grand vision, but in any case, one would have to say that Libra will undoubtedly become a 500-pound gorilla against which all other cryptocurrencies will ultimately get measured.

For those of you further interested in trying out Libra, there is a developers site known as the testnet, plus you'll want to come up-to-speed with the new programming language being introduced for Libra, known as Move.

The Move programming language and scripting allows for developing customized transaction processing logic and is a key to enabling the so-called "smart contracts" capability that robust versions of blockchain are known for.

Especially interesting, I believe, involves the ability to undertake "automatic proofs" to try and verify that a given transaction, such as a payment, presumably is being charged to solely the appropriate payer account and receiver account, and has no other inadvertent or indirect undesired and unintended consequences. That's an important mathematically hearty feature that is not routinely available by all entrants in this space.

There's a lot more to be said about the technical elements of Libra, which I'll cover it later posts, but the key business insights right now is to realize that:

- Facebook has around 2.38 billion active users, and thus if even a fraction of those users decides to embrace Libra, it will vault Libra into the cryptocurrency heavens.

- With Facebook and the other already known founding members being supporters of Libra, it has a push and energy-driving force unlike any that other entrants have ever seen.

- Given the backers and the prominence of Facebook, many consumers and businesses that have sat on the sidelines about using a cryptocurrency are bound to feel safer now to take a leap of faith and try it out, along with the likely ease of doing so via Facebook itself.

- In spite of what might seem like a potential dragon slayer in terms of knocking out other cryptocurrencies, it is conceivable that the legitimization and popularization due to Libra might actually help others, doing so in the classic saying that boats rise by the rising of the tide (though it certainly seems to be the case that Libra will suck-up a lot of the air in the room, you can bet on that).

- Recognizing the qualms that many have about by-faith-alone believing in many of the existent digital currencies that no particular backing in gold or some other kind of tangible asset, and appears to be a floating digital mirage, there will be a Libra Reserve, containing a "basket of bank deposits and short-term government securities" to underly the intrinsic value of the digital coinage (just to mention, some purists in this realm would decry this assets-backing approach as unpatriotic to the "true" vision of cryptocurrencies).

Self-Driving Cars And Blockchain And Cryptocurrencies

Amidst all the excitement about Libra, you might not have noticed that some of the founding members included entities that at initial glance might seem surprising to you, such as founding members of Uber and Lyft.

How did they get in there, you might be wondering?

The answer is pretty straightforward. If you are running a ridesharing or ride-hailing service, and you want to make life easy for your end-users that ride in your cars, providing them with a viable and reliable cryptocurrency couldn't hurt. Indeed, one might say it could help quite a bit. There are many riders that are bound to prefer using a cryptocurrency such as Libra, especially if it is easy to do.

Let's also consider the future, one composed of driverless autonomous cars.

I've long predicted that we'll see autonomous cars heavily leveraging blockchain and cryptocurrencies.

For a cryptocurrency, the uses are rather apparent, such as being able to pay your bill for having been a passenger in a driverless car. Another obvious example involves the autonomous car being able to pay tolls on roadways and bridges, doing so by electronically communicating with the toll taker, using V2I (vehicle-to-infrastructure) protocols.

For blockchain, upon which cryptocurrencies are built, the foundational platform can be used for other purposes besides just minting digital coins. The underlying blockchain could be used to keep track of the ownership record of the autonomous car, making it relatively easy to find out who bought the driverless car, when they did so, and who owns it now. Rather than keeping around tons of paperwork, this could be electronically stored and much more easily found and retrieved.

Another use of blockchain or DLT would be to keep track of the V2V (vehicle-to-vehicle) electronic communications. Conveying messages from driverless car to driverless car can be very handy, such as an autonomous car ahead of you that warns there is debris in the roadway or indicates that traffic is heavy, and you might want to pursue a different route.

The AI of autonomous cars will be carrying on dialogues during the driving journey, hopefully aiding each other in the process. Rather than these messages being amorphous and floating in the air, they could be codified into a DLT and then more readily shared or used (plus, you could add the cryptocurrency into this to offer financial incentives for having your driverless car share roadway statuses).

These examples and other "smart contracts" usages would all be spurred via using a blockchain or DLT capability.

Conclusion

Any ridesharing or ride-hailing service can see the writing on the wall, namely do whatever you can to keep close to your end-users and customers. Libra might be such a vehicle (pun intended).

I am anticipating that the automakers and tech firms that are developing autonomous cars will be likewise considering how to blend blockchain and cryptocurrency into their on-board systems, rather than letting others decide how to do so and either messing up the driving systems or creating a Rube Goldberg-like convoluted contortion.

From a zodiac sign perspective, the word Libra tends to mean something that is focused on symmetry, seeking to embrace equilibrium and doing so in terms of beauty, love, and money. Might the upstart, the Libra Association, be a Venus that brings us the symmetry and equilibrium that sparks a true breakout for wide adoption of cryptocurrency?

The signs sure seem to be pointing in that direction.

CHAPTER 13
SYSTEMS NAMING AND AI SELF-DRIVING CARS

CHAPTER 13
SYSTEMS NAMING AND AI SELF-DRIVING CARS

The news has been awash with raucous commentary about a recent study that attempted to analyze the names being given to various Advanced Driver Assistance Systems (ADAS), and unfortunately the preponderance of the blather is grossly misinterpreting what the study actually accomplished.

In particular, the most notable aspect involves the Autopilot name that has become a hallmark of Tesla and a favored moniker of Elon Musk.

In short, many are suggesting that the study purportedly "proves" that the Autopilot name is misleading and inappropriate, and that supposedly "drivers assume Autopilot does more than it does" (a matter that I'll be analyzing herein).

Some readers already know that I've taken to task Tesla and Musk for various aspects, including my analysis of their quarterly safety statistics, and for which I tried to provide a reasoned and thorough basis for asserting that those numbers are being misinterpreted, along with my expressed concern that Tesla essentially is promulgating the misinterpretations when it could readily be setting the record straight by providing more stats and sharing the underlying data to offer constructive validation and elaboration of their safety record (being more safety status transparent).

To put it mildly, some fans of Tesla were not particularly fond of the analysis. As such, I'm guessing that some of those same supporters might be surprised to see that I am now providing a kind of defense for Tesla on this recent news afront.

In our new-found era of tribalism, it seems that we all need to always be ensconced in one tribe or another. For Tesla, presumably you are either in the "always in favor" camp or you must otherwise be in the "always opposed" camp.

My camp is the one that seeks strong science and appropriate interpretations of scientific results.

This means that I'm ready, able, and purposeful about offering insights for circumstances that warrant being analyzed, regardless of which side the chips fall on. I am a proponent of properly conducted scientific studies, and an equally stout proponent of ensuring that those studies are interpreted sensibly and within the context of what the study actually shows.

Unpacking The Naming Study

Let's unpack what this naming study reported.

Researchers conducted a survey of about 2,000 drivers, nationally representative, via telephone, and the poll was performed in 2018.

It is useful to always first consider whom a survey targeted, how many respondents were involved, and how the survey respondents were selected.

I mention the importance of scrutinizing the sample set because there is the infamous case of the 1936 presidential election in which a reputable magazine predicted that candidate Alfred Landon would win over candidate Franklin D. Roosevelt, and the fatal flaw in that fouled prediction was that they used the telephone as the survey mechanism and yet in that particular time period only a certain class of people could afford phones, and therefore the case became a notable example of sampling bias.

I think we can be generally comfortable that the naming study's use of the telephone last year was satisfactory in today's times, and that 2,000 drivers is a large enough sample size of the overall population, and we'll take it at their word that they somehow were able to ensure that those contacted were a national representation of drivers.

You could easily skew such a study by either intentionally or unintentionally selecting only certain kinds of drivers, say only those over the age of 65, or you could focus on just drivers in the city of Pinole, but let's assume that didn't happen in this case.

What did the survey ask of the respondents?

Unfortunately, we aren't seemingly given the actual text of the questions used, and I'll just add that how you ask a question can make a big difference in the results of any survey, but in any case they reportedly asked "questions about behaviors respondents perceived as safe while a Level 2 driving automation systems is in operation."

As background, the Society for Automotive Engineers (SAE) has provided a multi-level numbering system to classify cars as to the extent of their automation.

The Level 4 and Level 5 are considered the topmost and would be essentially true autonomous cars, meaning there is no human driver needed, while the Level 3 and Level 2 are considered cars that require a human driver and involve a co-sharing of the driving task with the ADAS automation.

Be aware that I've described at length the difficulties associated with the co-sharing of automation and humans in the act of driving a car, especially as Level 3 is now emerging, and have forewarned that we are facing new dangers on our roadways as such.

Back to the study, the Autopilot name was "associated with the highest likelihood that drivers believed a behavior was safe while in operation, for every behavior measured, compared with other systems names. Many of these differences were statistically significant."

Furthermore, the study said that "when asked whether it would be safe to take one's hands off the wheel while using the technology, 48 percent of people asked about Autopilot said they thought it would be, compared with 33 percent or fewer for the other systems. Autopilot also had substantially greater proportions of people who thought it would be safe to look at scenery, read a book, talk on a cellphone or text."

It is also useful to mention that "each respondent was asked about two out of five system names at random for a balanced study design," of which the five system names were "Autopilot (used by Tesla), Traffic Jam Assist (Audi and Acura), Super Cruise (Cadillac), Driving Assistant Plus (BMW) and ProPilot Assist (Nissan)."

And, notably, "respondents also were asked about Level 2 systems in general and about their own vehicle and driving."

Finally, it is important to realize that "a limited proportion of drivers had experience with advanced driver assistance systems: 9–20% of respondents reported having at least one crash avoidance technology such as forward collision warning or lane departure warning, and fewer of these reported driving a vehicle in which Level 2 systems were available."

Making Conclusions Based On What The Study Did

Before I dig into what kinds of conclusions can be reached, let's start with how people can have misconceptions about all sorts of things in our world.

Surveys show that most people believe that bats are blind. Not so. Bats do have eyes and can see. Admittedly, bats do use echolocation, which is what most people think of when asked about bats, but nonetheless, bats are not blind.

Surveys show that most people believe that ostriches stick their heads into the sand to hide from their enemies. Not so. They often will flop to the ground and lay flat, but it would be quite extraordinary for one to try and bury its head.

My point being that people have tons of misconceptions, and yet the misconception might or might not particularly matter per se.

It seems to me that the respondents in the naming study generally had little if any experience using a Level 2 and less so any Level 3 cars, and so they were merely speculating about what the names of the ADAS might mean. Their concepts, whether right or wrong, whether on-target or off-target, appear to be based on conjecture.

I suppose it's not a good thing that a proportion of drivers have a misconception about Autopilot, and from a marketing perspective that they might have a false impression about what Autopilot can do, perhaps leading them to consider buying a Tesla when they don't really know what its capabilities are, but until those with these drivers with their misconceptions get behind the actual wheel of a Tesla, it's somewhat less crucial that they are harboring such misconceptions, in the balance of things.

In essence, this misconception about what Autopilot can or cannot do is really only crucial per se when it manifests itself in some substantive manner.

What we really need to know is whether such a misconception gets carried over into the act of driving a Tesla and using Autopilot.

Sure, there are anecdotal examples of Tesla drivers napping or doing other unsavory acts while needing to be undertaking the driving task, but until a quantitative study on that specific aspect is performed, the matter is still more anecdotal than substantiated in an evidentiary way.

For those that drive a Tesla and use Autopilot, if they misconceive what Autopilot can and cannot do, that's the danger spot. That's what we need to find out.

There is a long path between being someone that happens to drive cars, and having a misconception about Autopilot, and then putting that misconception into action.

Presumably, such a driver would need to get behind the wheel of a Tesla and be using Autopilot, in order for us to then have qualms about the facet that they don't know what they need to do as a driver and what the Autopilot is going to do.

Returning then to my earlier point, the chatter in the news is making the leap from the overall notion that drivers overall misconceive of what Autopilot does, and construing that this means that actual Autopilot-using drivers are full of misconceptions about Autopilot, for which we would all certainly be rightfully concerned.

The study does not say this, and nor was the study designed to get at this kind of question.

In my earlier indication, I said this:

In short, many are suggesting that the study purportedly "proves" that the Autopilot name is misleading and inappropriate, and that supposedly "drivers assume Autopilot does more than it does" (a matter that I'll be analyzing herein).

A key problem is that the word "drivers" is ambiguous, and it could be incorrectly construed as meaning "**Tesla** drivers assume Autopilot does more than it does" (I've inserted the word Tesla), but this study does not tackle that question, and instead the proper wording might be "**overall-drivers** assume that Autopilot does more than it does" (I've inserted the phrase overall-drivers, meaning drivers that generally aren't Tesla drivers and just so happen to drive cars of one kind or another).

That's a big distinction, a night and day difference.

Added Salient Points

I mentioned earlier herein that I was going to call things as I see them.

In terms of the recent study, I don't think its right to go beyond the nature of the study and make assertions that weren't under scrutiny. The study found that overall people, who happen to be drivers, seem to have misconceptions about Autopilot and assume that Autopilot can do more than it actually can do.

That makes sense to me, since I've always said that the Autopilot name is misleading in terms of what the automation currently can actually do.

It is perhaps helpful to know that my anecdotal belief is supported by the study and shows that people overall, consisting of drivers, in the United States, appear to have inflated views of Autopilot and that it might be because of the name (we don't know that it is the name per se, since it could also be that the respondents had some other way to reach this impression, but it seems fair game to assume it is the naming).

What we don't know from this particular study is whether or not those people that have inflated views of Autopilot are also then getting into a Tesla, turning on Autopilot, and driving on our public roadways with false assumptions, and for which it could cause them to get into car accidents and injure or kill others too.

Conclusion

Until we have robust studies that focus on that particular question, we are stuck with the intuitive sense that there are some Tesla drivers that have misconceptions about Autopilot, but we don't know how many and we don't know how often those such drivers are driving their Tesla's with Autopilot engaged.

There have been some related studies such as on human vigilance and Autopilot disengagements, and others, but the field is still wide open and more needs to be done.

We know for sure that some do have that misconception, as evidenced by the videos of Tesla drivers not properly performing the driving task while presumably Autopilot is on, yet we don't know how widespread this is. Of course, even just having a minor number of Tesla drivers doing so is dangerous, endangering themselves and the rest of us too.

In any case, it would be helpful to know how much a problem it is, the extent or magnitude, along with whether the various means to overcome it are in place and being appropriately undertaken. There are ongoing anecdotal remarks that some say showcase that Tesla drivers are informed about what Autopilot can do when they first get the car and thus do know what the limits of Autopilot are, while there are other equally voiced anecdotal remarks that there aren't any such trainings or that those trainings are done in a short shrift manner.

You can't really carry on much of a useful debate or discussion when all you have is a bunch of anecdotes. As they say, opinions are opinions, but having the facts makes for a better dialogue.

Well, as you can see, I appear to not be squarely in either tribe, neither the "always favors" Tesla and nor the "always opposes" Tesla.

Normally, the good thing about being in any particular tribe is that you usually get at least those tribe members to bolster you, supporting whatever you say, meanwhile the other opposing tribe is against you, but at least you've got a contingent backing you of the tribe you are in.

When you are not in either tribe, it usually means that both sides don't like what you say. Ouch!

In my defense, perhaps we could all agree that more needs to be done on this topic and it could benefit us all, no matter which side of the fence you happen to be sitting on.

In quick recap:

• *Easiest set:* Daylight, no traffic, open road, no weather, no pedestrians, smooth roads, definitive markings, pre-mapped, already driven, geofenced, no passenger instructions, snippet, one-act, unencumbered, ordinary encounters, and easy-going.

• *More challenging set:* Nighttime, claustrophobic traffic, complex convoluted roads, adverse weather, pedestrians galore, potholed roads, faded/no markings, partial/no mapping, first-time driven, open borders, passenger instructions, full journey, multi-acts, encumbered, edge case encounters, and crunch-oriented driving situations.

Next time you watch an autonomous car video, you be the judge.

CHAPTER 14

MID-TRAFFIC RENDEZVOUS AND AI SELF-DRIVING CARS

CHAPTER 14
MID-TRAFFIC RENDEZVOUS AND AI SELF-DRIVING CARS

Traffic on Los Angeles freeways is notorious for being stop-and-go, often trapping drivers in sluggish or at times an unmoving endless snarl of cars that are all vying for every cutthroat sought inch of progress they can make.

Driving a 20-mile commute at idealistic unimpeded freeway speeds should in-theory take around twenty to thirty minutes, yet the reality is that you can exasperatingly spend an hour to two hours trying to undertake such a relatively short-distance journey. Mostly, you are watching the bumper of a car ahead of you, typically just a few inches away, and the driver behind you is doing the same.

It is slow, pondering, agonizing, and frustrating when you know that your car can supposedly do zero to 60 in a few split seconds, yet your mechanical beast is being held back and kept to a slothful pace equivalent to a baby crawling along on all fours.

Hunger sometimes becomes an issue.

I was heading home from Burbank the other night and had planned on making a light supper in my kitchen.

Caught in onerous backed-up traffic, this time especially egregious due to a multi-car pile-up of cars that had occurred hours before but that was still immersed in the mopping up stage, I could hear my own stomach growling incessantly for attention.

My mind was trying to tell my hunger urge to wait until getting home, unfortunately the hunger craving was overpowering my mental resolve to holdout. I had skipped lunch at work because, well, there frequently just isn't time for lunch. My breakfast had been an energy bar and a bottled water, consumed during the morning commute to Burbank. Now, I was trapped in the middle of the freeway, had no food in the car, and was facing a lengthy delay getting to my food pantry.

I realize that starvation was not imminent, and I suppose that I shouldn't be carping about my hunger. Let's just agree that sometimes people while in their cars are bound to get hungry. Yes, I could have pulled off the freeway and done a drive-thru for some fast food, though I assure you that getting over to a freeway exit would have been a battle, plus the side streets were chocked with traffic, and then getting back onto the freeway would have been a tortuous wait since the entrance timers were on and timing car entries on an intermittent and eternity-long basis.

Traffic Jam Whopper To The Rescue

Burger King has found an answer to this stuck-in-traffic hunger problem, namely delivery of a combo meal of a burger, fries and a soda (or bottled water) directly to your car, while stranded in traffic jams.

After the famous restaurant chain had already tried this innovative service in Mexico City and found it successful, they are now aiming to do the same in Los Angeles, opting to call the new service *The Traffic Jam Whopper*.

Here's how it works.

While driving in your car, you use a special mobile app on your smartphone to place the order. The order is shunted to a nearby Burger King restaurant, which prepares your meal, and then a motorcyclist is dispatched to your location.

Your location is ascertained via the GPS coordinates provided by your smartphone, and the motorcyclist then attempts to find your car in the morass of vehicles on the freeway (your app setup provided added info such as the make and model, color, and other facets of your car). The motorcyclist pulls alongside your car, you open your car window, and the motorcyclist passes your bagged combo and drink to you. No need to pay the motorcyclist directly since the mobile app charges your credit card.

What makes this viable is that motorcyclists in California can do lane splitting, meaning that a motorcycle can go between lanes and weave its way throughout traffic. As such, in spite of enormous miles-long lines of cars, motorcyclists typically move ahead at a rapid clip (though, let's be clear, this is a dicey activity, and I've seen many motorcyclists that landed head-first on the paved road as a result of a car suddenly shifting in a lane).

I'm guessing that many of you are right away decrying this notion of fast food delivery while in the middle of traffic as an unimaginable form of lunacy, or maybe even worse a potential new way for getting people killed. Some might say it is an "innovation" and invitation for injury and death, rather than being simply a novel means of fast food delivery.

Aren't drivers already distracted enough?

Now, they need to be watching for additional motorcyclists, they need to be watching for cars that are trying to align with a motorcyclist and pass food between them, etc.

It sure seems like this might produce even more bumper-to-bumper rear enders than we already have. The slower speeds of snarled traffic do make this less likely to lead to actual deaths, and presumably milder injuries, yet it still seems to smack the rails of sensibility the wrong way.

And, by the way, will this speed-up traffic (no, of course not!), so it is really a potential boon to making a lousy traffic situation even lousier. You might argue it is a self-fulfilling prophecy, a person orders and gets their burger, slowing down traffic further, others get hungry due to the longer time in traffic, so they order a burger, and the cycle feeds upon itself. Clever for the fast food business!

If you are concerned that the driver placing such an order will be distracted, Burger King is so far indicating that the orders are placed only by voice command, thus the ordering driver does not have to apparently text and drive (and no-no worthy of a ticket in California), and the order itself is limited to the combo meal only, reducing any back-and-forth dialogue that might require further human attention.

Whether you are outraged at this service, or you find it amusing, or you are tempted to try it, I'm not going to further address herein the utility of it and will instead use it as a springboard for another related topic.

Upon the advent of self-driving driverless cars, you can expect that mid-traffic delivery between autonomous cars is likely to arise and become a somewhat popular activity.

Allow me to unpack that statement.

Self-Driving Cars And Coordinated On-Road Interactions

At some point in the future, we'll presumably have truly autonomous cars on our public roadways, roaming freely and eventually becoming the predominant way of getting around (human driven cars gradually receding and no longer kept in use). Autonomous or driverless cars do not require and nor even allow for a human driver and instead are driven entirely and solely by an AI system.

To clarify, I'm not suggesting this advent is going to happen anytime soon, and I've repeatedly emphasized that we are a long way afar of such a day.

In any case, once we do reach that status, it does open the possibility of doing "tricky" driving that we today would generally find reprehensible in human based driving. Open your mind to a time when the ways of human drivers are no longer dominant.

Self-driving driverless cars will be employing V2V (vehicle-to-vehicle) electronic communications. This allows the AI systems of autonomous cars to electronically chat with each other. Trying to get one driverless car to rendezvous with another driverless car will be relatively easy to do, since they can both be communicating across an online network and be navigating toward each other.

I've written and spoken previously about the various new types of car caravans and motorcades that will be possible as a result of driverless cars. Whereas today it is usually arduous to try and coordinate a multitude of cars during their driving journey, the use of autonomous cars and coupled with V2V is going to make it a snap to do.

The Burger King example using human driven cars and human driven motorcycles is perhaps an earlier form of allowing for mid-traffic interactions among vehicles. Today, it certainly seems like a rather dicey proposition.

With driverless cars, assuming they are otherwise safe to be on our roads, the added element of them coordinating and aligning with each other mid-traffic is not much of an added effort.

On a related topic, in an earlier piece I had discussed the aspect of upcoming capabilities of deliveries to the trunk of your car, an emerging service that would have packages placed into the trunk of your parked car, doing so while you are say at work and your car is sitting in a nearby parking lot. This is another kind of service that could be ratcheted up via autonomous cars, allowing a transfer of a package into another autonomous car, either while one is parked and stationary, or while both are underway and in traffic.

Of course, such driverless cars would need to be designed to accommodate these kinds of in-motion transfers.

The trunk that you know of today might be differently shaped and opened, allowing for a slot into which a package could be inserted, and the slot or door then closed to keep the package inside. This could also be a means to deliver fast food, entering into the slot, and then moved into the body of the autonomous car where the passengers are sitting.

In the case of the Burger King delivery, there needs to be a human in the car to receive the fast food. With driverless cars, it could be that your autonomous car picks up your food for you, while on an errand, not even needing to swing into a fast food eatery, and instead gets the fast food while on-the-go and then brings it to you at home or work.

This also dovetails into my piece describing tryouts underway by Uber of delivering McDonald's fast food via autonomous drones, doing so by delivering initially to human driven cars and then later on progressing to doing so to autonomous cars. A driverless car might allow for vehicle-to-vehicle transfers, along with drone-to-car transfers.

In case you are wondering about the motorcyclist aspects, perhaps puzzled about whether humans will be riding motorcycles in the midst of droves of driverless cars, though it is conceivable that humans will still be able to ride their motorcycles in such situations, there is also work underway to create driverless motorcycles.

Thus, it is probably more likely that a future equivalent to the Burger King effort would consist of a delivery by a driverless motorcycle to a driverless car, and into the hands of a human or humans inside the autonomous car, or the food would be carted by the driverless car to wherever the ordering human resides.

Conclusion

I don't want to leave you with an impression that the mid-traffic and in-motion transfer operations are going to be error free, even in an era of predominantly autonomous vehicles.

There are still chances of things going awry. There will be risks of the vehicles having something go wrong at the wrong moments, and there is always the chance of say debris on the roadway that could foul-up such operations.

Meanwhile, I suppose we'll need to see how the human version of mid-traffic and in-motion transfers plays out.

It also makes one wonder, if your stomach is growling and you just have to eat something, do you think that you could flag that fast food motorcyclist coming past you to transfer the food to your car, instead of the ordering car, perhaps for a really generous tip?

Maybe that's not proper mid-traffic in-motion transfer etiquette (what would Miss Manners espouse?).

CHAPTER 15
PAIRING DRONES AND AI SELF-DRIVING CARS

CHAPTER 15
PAIRING DRONES AND AI SELF-DRIVING CARS

Look in the sky, it's a bird, it's a plane, no, it is an autonomous drone. Not just any autonomous drone, but one carrying a freshly cooked juicy hamburger and some mouth-watering crispy French fries.

Meanwhile, please look down there at the road below, is it a speeding locomotive, no, it's a self-driving driverless car that is going to be the landing pad for the fast food carrying driverless drone.

I've now described for you the approach being tested by several major companies that are embarking upon speeding up the delivery of fast food to your home or business.

The idea is that the fast food restaurant cooks your requested meal, they then place it into an autonomous drone, the drone flies rapidly to an autonomous car that is nearby your home or business, lands on the autonomous car, and the autonomous car then finishes the delivery journey by driving up to your door.

Recently, Uber got in the news for its initial tryouts in San Diego, California, taking baby steps toward this overarching approach, and will this summer be advancing their efforts even further with its initial partner, McDonalds restaurants. You might say that Uber Eats and Uber Elevate are moving us into the space age, which just about all other food delivery services are also hopeful of doing.

Rather than the conventional method of using a human driver that picks up your meal at the local McDonalds and drives it to you, the aim is to have an autonomous drone be the pick-up and also speedily get the meal reasonably close to your destination, leaving the last dollop of remaining distance for the driverless car to finish the delivery.

According to their earlier trials, Uber claims that the drone usage will cut the 21 minutes for an all ground-based driven method of covering a 1.5-mile distance to instead be about 7 minutes, thus shaving two-thirds of the delivery time. Presumably, you will be happier to get your ordered meal into your hungry hands sooner, plus the recently cooked meal is more likely to still be in its pristine juicy and crispy state.

Let's unpack some of the salient elements of this autonomous pairing, namely the jointly tasked and coordinated efforts of autonomous drones with autonomous cars.

Why Use Such High-Tech For Fast Food Delivery

First, I'm sure that some of you are vexed about using the sophistication of high-tech drones as coupled with the sophistication of high-tech driverless cars to simply deliver a Big Mac to your door. Of all of the important things to be done on this planet and for our world, does being able to more quickly deliver fast food qualify as a basis for utilizing the most advanced technology that can be created?

Well, given that the food delivery industry is forecasted to rise to about $76 billion by the year 2022, I guess you could say the answer is yes, indeedy do, as it makes indubitable profitable sense to exploit whatever technology you can find or craft in order to grab part of those massive delivery bucks beckoning to be spent.

Of course, the delivery payload does not need to be fast food. You could use the same arrangement to deliver medicines to those that are in vital need, such as the efforts of the company Zipline doing so in Rwanda. The payload could consist of critically needed blood supplies, or might have vaccines that are being used to combat a spreading malady.

Depending upon the size of the drones being used for delivery, the same approach could be used to deliver packages and parcels. There has been a lot of reporting about trials underway by UPS, USPS, Amazon, and many other logistics and transport companies that see the future involving drones overhead to get goods from point A to point B.

My overall point is that it is prudent to pursue the drones and driving approach for delivery and you can then choose what kinds of items to deliver.

In a sense, deliver whatever you can at first, providing an opportunity to perfect the tech and the approach, which ultimately once the kinks are ironed out you can then use for a multitude of purposes. Fast food delivery offers a twofer, it will make money as a delivery mechanism and it will advance the ability to enact deliveries in this fashion.

Does Autonomy Make A Difference

The next point you might be pondering is whether it is necessary to use an autonomous drone, officially referred to as an Unmanned Aerial Vehicle (UAV), and whether it is necessary to use an autonomous car, which is another kind of Autonomous Vehicle (AV).

Nope, you don't need to have autonomy baked into all of this.

You could have a manned drone that is controlled by a human operator. You could have the manned drone flown to a manned car. The human driver in the car would then finish driving the final distance to the indicated destination. All of the human labor though is going to push-up your costs to do the delivery. You also would need to deal with being able to hire the needed labor, and cope with all of the other human resources elements that accompany having humans-in-the-loop.

Most are betting that the human out-of-the-loop will be cheaper than having humans in-the-loop.

In theory, you also can cut down on the chances of human error, such as the operator of the drone getting careless and flying the drone to the wrong place, or the human driver in the car having fallen asleep doesn't awaken once the food has been delivered to the car. Autonomy, once properly established, would do away with those qualms, though of course introduces other aspects such as the need to keep the autonomous systems up-to-date and monitored.

Does The Car Need To Be Included

So far, I've hopefully conveyed that it makes sense that there would be a drone involved in the delivery, and this begs another question about whether it is needed to have a car involved too.

Why not just have the drone directly deliver the fast food to the final destination, rather than to a car?

The issue with delivering directly to a destination such as a home would be the matter of how to get the payload into the hands of the person that ordered the meal.

You could have the drone land in the backyard or front yard of a home, which many are experimenting with, but this is a dicey proposition since the yard might be cluttered and there isn't a viable and safe spot to land on. Or, maybe the yard has a dog that isn't going to favor a foreign craft that comes into the animal's turf. Someone or something can get hurt by the landing drone.

If landing the drone into a yard isn't good, some have attempted to use a cable that would gradually lower the payload from the drone, keeping the drone hovering and off the ground, and thus allow the person to get their meal or package by plucking it from the end of the cable. This has its own downsides, including that you now have a hovering drone, which is not good for various reasons, and the cable and its payload can become a potential swinging bat that could hit or harm someone or something.

All in all, you would want to have the drone land someplace that is safe and secure. Voila, use the top of a car. You could have a designated car that is especially equipped for a drone to land on the top of the car, and the car could then proceed to drive to the final destination. This gives you a guaranteed landing spot, and one without the other issues of landing in a yard or dangling the payload.

More About The Autonomous Car As The Landing Zone

Alright, so we'll use an autonomous car for this purpose, which provides a handy, secure, and safe landing spot, and we won't use a human driver, partially to cut down on the costs involved in the delivery process. You'll see in a moment that there are additional reasons to remove the human driver from this equation.

Where will the autonomous car be?

That's a good question.

The delivery process is behooved by trying to get the autonomous car as close to the final destination as feasible, thereby reducing the driving time portion of the journey. The autonomous car could park on the street, perhaps in front of the home or down the street from the home, though this might not be a clear and safe enough place to land the drone.

Suppose the street involved has a beautiful canopy formed by lush trees on both sides of the street. Bad news for trying to land the drone. There might be power lines and telephone poles. Etc. As such, the autonomous car might go park itself in an empty parking lot, wait for the drone to arrive, have the drone land, and then proceed to the final destination.

Generally, once the drone lands on the car, there's not much of a need to keep the drone there, and thus it would disgorge its payload and then likely lift-off right away. I say right away because the drone is really only a money maker whenever it is in the act of delivery. No sense in having it sit on the top of the car when it can be rushing onward to get the next newly cooked chicken sandwich and onion rings that a starving customer is eagerly awaiting.

Some Added Details About The Autonomous Car

There are some very interesting logistical problems that come to play in this drone and driving delivery method.

Imagine that you have a fleet of autonomous cars.

You might dedicate some of the autonomous cars to being solely for delivery purposes, but this then restricts the opportunities to make money with those driverless cars so allocated. It might be better to have your autonomous cars available as ridesharing or ride-haling vehicles, and also equip them to handle the food delivery aspects, such as having specialized equipment mounted on the car to allow for the drone landings.

Here's the tricky part. You want to keep your autonomous cars roaming to do ridesharing. When an autonomous drone delivery is imminent, you want to detect which of your driverless cars is closest to the final destination, one that hasn't been tagged as yet for a pending ridesharing request, and for which any of those candidate available driverless cars can also best get to a place to park that will be suitable to allow the drone to land and then take-off.

You'll need some pretty clever algorithms and routing software to figure this out. I make this point to emphasize that the autonomous drone and the autonomous car aren't the only "systems" elements of this delivery process, and there needs to be the "glue" that aids the drone and car in coordinating their efforts. More AI to be had, I'd wager.

Lots Of Aspects To Sort Through

The Federal Aviation Administration (FAA) is in the driver's seat on these matters due to the drones being involved, including requiring that any companies using drones for delivery must get an FAA designated Air Carrier Certification. There is an overall program known as the Unmanned Aircraft System (UAS) Integration Pilot Program (IPP), currently governing the various tryouts and trials that companies such as Uber are undertaking.

Driverless cars also have their own set of regulations, somewhat, as per the states allowing autonomous cars on their public roadways.

To avoid having drones flying and crisscrossing over dense urban and city areas, the pairing of autonomous drones with autonomous cars makes a lot of sense, allowing the driverless drone to be routed in a means to minimize its time over populated areas and then rendezvous with a driverless car that's awaiting the receiving of the payload.

Could the autonomous car be in-motion when rendezvousing with the driverless drone, rather than being parked? Yes, that's a definite possibility and could shorten further the time needed to make the final delivery, though it introduces other facets.

Would a moving driverless car that is being approached by a drone be somewhat startling to human drivers that might be in nearby cars? Imagine you are on the freeway, driving your car, and all of a sudden a drone swoops down from the clouds and lands on the autonomous car in front of you. Doubtful that human drivers would not react adversely to the matter.

Likewise, this is another reason to have the autonomous car rather than use a human to drive the drone receiving car, since a human driving a car might not be as adept at timing the landing of the drone, whereas a driverless car could be electronically in communication with the drone to align for the landing and take-off actions.

Conclusion

Societal questions are being asked about how safe are the drones, since an autonomous drone might go awry and crash into someone or something, doing so while on a journey to deliver a burger, and one would right away wonder whether the damage or injuries were worth the desire to get fast food into someone's hands.

Where will the autonomous car be when the drone attempts to land is another big question. Suppose the autonomous car chooses to park in a school parking lot, and moments later the kids are let out of class because the school day has ended. Do you want a driverless drone coming to land onto a parked autonomous car in a school zone? Probably not.

As per the FAA USA IPP, we all need to undertake a meaningful dialogue about how to balance everyone's interests on such matters.

Once we've figured that out, I guess the only questions leftover will be whether to order the burger or the fish sandwich.

CHAPTER 16

LOST WALLET STUDY AND AI SELF-DRIVING CARS

CHAPTER 16
LOST WALLET STUDY AND AI SELF-DRIVING CARS

Recent news stories have been touting how honest we all are, as evidenced by a large-scale experiment that involved the use of faked lost wallets.

Many have said that the study conclusively showed a seemingly counterintuitive result, namely that people were "more honest" when a lost wallet had more money in it, apparently showcasing a sense of altruism, along with a personal aversion toward feeling as though they themselves were a thief.

As a headline grabber, the study and the interpretation of the results certainly provides a feel-good sensation and likely brightens our day as a humanity.

That being said, though I don't want to rain on the happiness about honesty parade, I think it might be helpful to take a closer look at the study and make sure that the popular interpretation is appropriate.

Readers of my column are aware that I've previously tackled research studies done in the self-driving and driverless car realm, and offered that we should be cautious in taking at face value any published study and the concomitant interpretation that oftentimes becomes the soundbite conveying what the study means and how to use its results.

Let's unpack the wallet study, shall we.

Background About the Wallet Study Experiment

Researchers decided that it would be insightful to conduct a kind of social experiment to try and ascertain civic honesty, doing so on a widespread basis not previously undertaken. In this case, they used over a dozen research assistants that fanned out to over 40 countries, 355 major cities, and involved over 17,000 unsuspecting subjects into the experiment, taking place over a roughly three-year time span.

Here's what they did.

Faked wallets were prepared and the research assistants would go into a place of business, find an employee that seemed to be at a reception desk or equivalent, and would hurriedly hand the employee the wallet, explaining that the wallet had been found outside around the corner, doing so using this script: "Hi, I found this [showing the wallet] on the street just around the corner. Somebody must have lost it. I'm in a hurry and have to go. Can you please take care of it?"

The research assistant would try to push the wallet toward the employee, hoping that the employee would essentially take possession of the wallet, and then the researcher got out of the vicinity as quickly as possible so as to avoid being asked any questions about the wallet or the circumstances thereof. Unwittingly, the employee becomes an experimental subject, and the research assistant is presumably able to pull this off without tipping the employee that anything is untoward.

Of the businesses that the researchers chose, they reported that 23% were banks, 14% were post offices, 22% were hotels, 21% were public offices such as police stations and courts of law, and 20% were cultural establishments.

The faked wallets were somewhat unusual in that they were actually transparent oversized business card cases, which was used to enable the subjects to readily see the contents without having to actually open the wallet per se. Within the faked wallets were three identical business cards, each containing the name, title, and email address of presumably the wallet owner (this was faked by the researchers), and had a grocery list, a key, and possibly some cash.

For the experimental treatment, the researchers were aiming to alter the amount of cash in various wallets to discern whether the magnitude of the included cash would impact the likelihood of the subjects opting to try and contact the presumed wallet owner, which the only means to do so would be via the email address shown on the business cards (note that there wasn't a telephone number on the business cards, nor a mailing address, thus limiting the means by which the wallet owner could be contacted).

There were three categories of the cash magnitude: (i) the NoMoney category in which there was no cash in the faked wallet, (ii) the Money category that had $13.45 in the wallet, and (iii) the BigMoney category that had $94.15 in cash inside the wallet.

According to the researchers, it turns out that in the NoMoney category there were 40% that attempted to contact the wallet owner, and the Money category had 51% that tried to contact the wallet owner, while the BigMoney category had 72% that tried to contact the wallet owner.

From these results, most seem to conclude that since the BigMoney category had the highest percentage of attempts to reach the wallet owner, it is a "surprising" result since you would expect that if people were generally tending toward being dishonest they would seek to pocket the BigMoney and not contact the wallet owner, and presumably would be more likely to contact the wallet owner when there was NoMoney since there wasn't anything to steal.

That's how the headlines have come to claiming that we all are apparently more honest than might have been assumed, and that we seem to also be personally motivated via a nagging feeling that if we don't do the honest act then we must be a thief and our consciences won't tolerate it.

I suppose you could try to reach that conclusion, but it seems to leave out a lot of other equally fitting explanations.

Unpacking The Wallet Study Aspects

One of the biggest concerns that I see about the study approach was that contrary to what the news media says, it was not a study of overall civic honesty because it purposely narrowed the nature of the subjects being drawn into the experiment.

The subjects were presumably employees of businesses or entities of one kind or another. They were made unwitting participants while on-the-job.

I point this out because it would seem a far cry from say randomly going up to people on the street or in a park and getting them to become subjects in the experiment. That might be a more applicable way to try and aim at the general population.

Instead, the research involved people employed that were at their workplace, and for which I submit the results would potentially differ from doing the same kind of experiment for anyone in the open public (or, let me put it this way, trying to generalize from the study to suggest that all people would do the same as the subjects in this experiment seems, well, overreaching).

Sampling bias is an important matter to any study.

One of the most famous examples of how a sampling bias can misshape a study involves the matter of a telephone survey in 1936 that conducted a poll of whom voters were going to most likely choose for the U.S. presidency, and the poll results got it quite wrong. This was attributed to the aspect that at that time period the only people that could afford phones were not a cross-representation of the American voters.

In the wallet study, the employees were working at their job and so might have perceived a greater need to take action about the lost wallet, not because of any personal sense of altruistic honesty per se, but due to the fact that they encountered the situation while at work. The researchers tried to deal with this facet somewhat by trying to note if there were any cameras or other eyewitnesses, but I contend that even if there wasn't any such monitoring, the employee still has a sense of duty to their employer and their desire to keep their job.

The researchers suggest that by telling the subjects that the wallet was found outside and around the corner that the subject would feel at ease, as though it would be unlikely that the owner might come looking for the wallet. Thus, presumably, the employee is relieved of any chance of being named as having received the wallet.

Not quite.

This brings me to the next concern, specifically that the experimenters themselves could be considered as shaping the results, without realizing they are doing so.

Though the wallet owner might or might not show-up, the research assistant is indeed a witness to the act of providing the wallet to the employee. At some later point, as far as the employee knows, the research assistant might return and ask whether the employee had ever done anything about the wallet or could attest that they gave the wallet to the employee.

Once again, this ties back to the workplace element. The subject can be found again, and has presumably a want to keep their job, thus they might be more so motivated to take action about the wallets.

Again, this is quite different than if you found a wallet on the street or in a park, by yourself. You'd likely pick-up the wallet, look around to see if someone nearby might be the owner, or might be a witness to your picking up the wallet. Nobody though knows who you are. In the case of the wallet study, the subjects that they work at company X and work at the reception or similar area can be ultimately retraced, and they know it.

In the case of this faked wallet study it has contrived a built-in witness, the research assistant. I realize that the study assumes that the employee assumes that the research assistant was just wandering in and won't ever return, but I wonder if that's really what the employees imagined.

As an anecdotal example, the other day I was at a restaurant waiting to be seated, when a person came up to the hostess and explained they had lost their car keys, had been standing around in the parking lot trying to find them, when another person came up and explained they had found the keys and given them to the hostess in the restaurant, including describing what the hostess looked like. Though it was the owner that came to get the keys, my point is that the person that turned in the keys was a witness of having given the keys to the employee.

More Qualms About The Study Interpretation

Another element that seems worthy of attention involves the money amounts.

The media led with the headline that the more money involved, the more honest someone becomes. This needs to be clarified, I believe.

As mentioned, the study used either no money in the wallet, or $13.45, or $94.15 in the wallet. I'm not so sure that we can really call the $94.15 as being "big money" in any overall sense. Yes, the $94.15 is more than the $13.45, but let's all agree (I believe) that something around $100 is not necessarily the same as if the wallet had $1,000 or had $10,000 in it, or $100,000 in it (just being a bit provocative since I realize that stuffing $100,000 into the wallet would be rather difficult to do).

Does the amount of money tie to the "civic honesty" factor or might it really be more connected to the job repercussions aspects?

If your manager comes to you and asks what did you do about some wallet that was given to you in a lost-and-found manner, and the wallet had a substantive dollar amount, you'd likely look worse if you hadn't tried to contact the wallet owner. For a wallet that had nothing of value, you could always say that it had no money and therefore you just sat on the matter and took no action. In contrast, if the wallet had any substantive money in it, you'd look like you were negligent in not trying to get it back to the owner.

Furthermore, you could possibly be accused of taking the money from the wallet and also the odds are that perhaps the wallet owner will try to come and find the wallet, or maybe even the witness (the research assistant) might return to try and claim it. All of those possibilities might get weighed in the mind of the employee. Given that they could possibly lose their job for not taking action or having other accusations made, it would tend to behoove them to do something, especially when the money amount gets higher.

Not wanting to seem to be a downer about honesty, but suppose the wallet did contain $100,000, which presumably would be a huge amount and something beyond the job pay of the employee.

In that case, there might be quite a mental tussle by the employee as to whether they can pocket the truly big money, though at the risk of losing their job (but it might be worth it for the money involved), versus the risk that the wallet owner or the witness would try to come and find the wallet.

Essentially, even if you buy into the idea that a person will be more honest as the amount of money rises, does their become some threshold at which the "honesty" gives way to the dollars involved as being so tempting that honesty no longer holds?

Conclusion

I certainly don't want to quash your hopes that people are honest, maybe they are, but I think that whenever any research study is undertaken it becomes important to step beyond the headlines.

In the self-driving driverless car realm, I had previously pointed out that the driving record of those driving a particular brand of car might differ from the driving practices of the general population because of the sampling selection involved.

In the case of Tesla's, at this juncture the buyers are able to afford a more expensive car than is the average car, and they are early adopters, all of which makes them potentially unlike the general population of drivers.

I've used the wallet study to illuminate ways in which you can look underneath the hood about any research study that pops into the popular press and catches the eye of the world. What is the sampling method used? How was the effort undertaken? What explanations and alternative explanations can be made? And so on.

We need to make sure that we have our eyes wide open and honestly give a close scrubbing to whatever news we're being fed.

APPENDIX

APPENDIX A
TEACHING WITH THIS MATERIAL

The material in this book can be readily used either as a supplemental to other content for a class, or it can also be used as a core set of textbook material for a specialized class. Classes where this material is most likely used include any classes at the college or university level that want to augment the class by offering thought provoking and educational essays about AI and self-driving cars.

In particular, here are some aspects for class use:

- Computer Science. Studying AI, autonomous vehicles, etc.
- Business. Exploring technology and it adoption for business.
- Sociology. Sociological views on the adoption and advancement of technology.

Specialized classes at the undergraduate and graduate level can also make use of this material.

For each chapter, consider whether you think the chapter provides material relevant to your course topic. There is plenty of opportunity to get the students thinking about the topic and force them to decide whether they agree or disagree with the points offered and positions taken. I would also encourage you to have the students do additional research beyond the chapter material presented (I provide next some suggested assignments they can do).

RESEARCH ASSIGNMENTS ON THESE TOPICS

Your students can find background material on these topics, doing so in various business and technical publications. I list below the top ranked AI related journals. For business publications, I would suggest the usual culprits such as the Harvard Business Review, Forbes, Fortune, WSJ, and the like.

Here are some suggestions of homework or projects that you could assign to students:

a) Assignment for foundational AI research topic: Research and prepare a paper and a presentation on a specific aspect of Deep AI, Machine Learning, ANN, etc. The paper should cite at least 3 reputable sources. Compare and contrast to what has been stated in this book.

b) Assignment for the Self-Driving Car topic: Research and prepare a paper and Self-Driving Cars. Cite at least 3 reputable sources and analyze the characterizations. Compare and contrast to what has been stated in this book.

c) Assignment for a Business topic: Research and prepare a paper and a presentation on businesses and advanced technology. What is hot, and what is not? Cite at least 3 reputable sources. Compare and contrast to the depictions in this book.

d) Assignment to do a Startup: Have the students prepare a paper about how they might startup a business in this realm. They must submit a sound Business Plan for the startup. They could also be asked to present their Business Plan and so should also have a presentation deck to coincide with it.

You can certainly adjust the aforementioned assignments to fit to your particular needs and the class structure. You'll notice that I ask for 3 reputable cited sources for the paper writing based assignments. I usually steer students toward "reputable" publications, since otherwise they will cite some oddball source that has no credentials other than that they happened to write something and post it onto the Internet. You can define "reputable" in whatever way you prefer, for example some faculty think Wikipedia is not reputable while others believe it is reputable and allow students to cite it.

The reason that I usually ask for at least 3 citations is that if the student only does one or two citations they usually settle on whatever they happened to find the fastest. By requiring three citations, it usually seems to force them to look around, explore, and end-up probably finding five or more, and then whittling it down to 3 that they will actually use.

I have not specified the length of their papers, and leave that to you to tell the students what you prefer. For each of those assignments, you could end-up with a short one to two pager, or you could do a dissertation length paper. Base the length on whatever best fits for your class, and the credit amount of the assignment within the context of the other grading metrics you'll be using for the class.

I mention in the assignments that they are to do a paper and prepare a presentation. I usually try to get students to present their work. This is a good practice for what they will do in the business world. Most of the time, they will be required to prepare an analysis and present it. If you don't have the class time or inclination to have the students present, then you can of course cut out the aspect of them putting together a presentation.

If you want to point students toward highly ranked journals in AI, here's a list of the top journals as reported by *various citation counts sources* (this list changes year to year):

- Communications of the ACM
- Artificial Intelligence
- Cognitive Science
- IEEE Transactions on Pattern Analysis and Machine Intelligence
- Foundations and Trends in Machine Learning
- Journal of Memory and Language
- Cognitive Psychology
- Neural Networks
- IEEE Transactions on Neural Networks and Learning Systems
- IEEE Intelligent Systems
- Knowledge-based Systems

GUIDE TO USING THE CHAPTERS

For each of the chapters, I provide next some various ways to use the chapter material. You can assign the tasks as individual homework assignments, or the tasks can be used with team projects for the class. You can easily layout a series of assignments, such as indicating that the students are to do item "a" below for say Chapter 1, then "b" for the next chapter of the book, and so on.

a) What is the main point of the chapter and describe in your own words the significance of the topic,

b) Identify at least two aspects in the chapter that you agree with, and support your concurrence by providing at least one other outside researched item as support; make sure to explain your basis for disagreeing with the aspects,

c) Identify at least two aspects in the chapter that you disagree with, and support your disagreement by providing at least one other outside researched item as support; make sure to explain your basis for disagreeing with the aspects,

d) Find an aspect that was not covered in the chapter, doing so by conducting outside research, and then explain how that aspect ties into the chapter and what significance it brings to the topic,

e) Interview a specialist in industry about the topic of the chapter, collect from them their thoughts and opinions, and readdress the chapter by citing your source and how they compared and contrasted to the material,

f) Interview a relevant academic professor or researcher in a college or university about the topic of the chapter, collect from them their thoughts and opinions, and readdress the chapter by citing your source and how they compared and contrasted to the material,

g) Try to update a chapter by finding out the latest on the topic, and ascertain whether the issue or topic has now been solved or whether it is still being addressed, explain what you come up with.

The above are all ways in which you can get the students of your class involved in considering the material of a given chapter. You could mix things up by having one of those above assignments per each week, covering the chapters over the course of the semester or quarter.

As a reminder, here are the chapters of the book and you can select whichever chapters you find most valued for your particular class:

Chapter Title

1 Eliot Framework for AI Self-Driving Cars

2 Essential Stats and AI Self-Driving Cars

3 Stats Fallacies and AI Self-Driving Cars

4 Driver Bullies and AI Self-Driving Cars

5 Sunday Drives and AI Self-Driving Cars

6 Face Recog Bans and AI Self-Driving Cars

7 States On-The-Hook and AI Self-Driving Cars

8 Sensors Profiting and AI Self-Driving Cars

9 Unruly Riders and AI Self-Driving Cars

10 Father's Day and AI Self-Driving Cars

11 Summons Feature and AI Self-Driving Cars

12 Libra Cryptocurrency and AI Self-Driving Cars

13 Systems Naming and AI Self-Driving Cars

14 Mid-Traffic Rendezvous and AI Self-Driving Cars

15 Pairing Drones and AI Self-Driving Cars

16 Lost Wallet Study and AI Self-Driving Cars

Companion Book By This Author

Advances in AI and Autonomous Vehicles: Cybernetic Self-Driving Cars

Practical Advances in Artificial Intelligence (AI) and Machine Learning

by

Dr. Lance B. Eliot, MBA, PhD

Chapter Title

1 Genetic Algorithms for Self-Driving Cars
2 Blockchain for Self-Driving Cars
3 Machine Learning and Data for Self-Driving Cars
4 Edge Problems at Core of True Self-Driving Cars
5 Solving the Roundabout Traversal Problem for SD Cars
6 Parallel Parking Mindless Task for SD Cars: Step It Up
7 Caveats of Open Source for Self-Driving Cars
8 Catastrophic Cyber Hacking of Self-Driving Cars
9 Conspicuity for Self-Driving Cars
10 Accident Scene Traversal for Self-Driving Cars
11 Emergency Vehicle Awareness for Self-Driving Cars
12 Are Left Turns Right for Self-Driving Cars
13 Going Blind: When Sensors Fail on Self-Driving Cars
14 Roadway Debris Cognition for Self-Driving Cars
15 Avoiding Pedestrian Roadkill by Self-Driving Cars
16 When Accidents Happen to Self-Driving Cars
17 Illegal Driving for Self-Driving Cars
18 Making AI Sense of Road Signs
19 Parking Your Car the AI Way
20 Not Fast Enough: Human Factors in Self-Driving Cars
21 State of Government Reporting on Self-Driving Cars
22 The Head Nod Problem for Self-Driving Cars
23 CES Reveals Self-Driving Car Differences

Companion Book By This Author

Self-Driving Cars:
"The Mother of All AI Projects"

by Dr. Lance B. Eliot, MBA, PhD

Chapter Title

1 Grand Convergence Explains Rise of Self-Driving Cars
2 Here is Why We Need to Call Them Self-Driving Cars
3 Richter Scale for Levels of Self-Driving Cars
4 LIDAR as Secret Sauce for Self-Driving Cars
5 Pied Piper Approach to SD Car-Following
6 Sizzle Reel Trickery for AI Self-Driving Car Hype
7 Roller Coaster Public Perception of Self-Driving Cars
8 Brainless Self-Driving Shuttles Not Same as SD Cars
9 First Salvo Class Action Lawsuits for Defective SD Cars
10 AI Fake News About Self-Driving Cars
11 Rancorous Ranking of Self-Driving Cars
12 Product Liability for Self-Driving Cars
13 Humans Colliding with Self-Driving Cars
14 Elderly Boon or Bust for Self-Driving Cars
15 Simulations for Self-Driving Cars: Machine Learning
16 DUI Drunk Driving by Self-Driving Cars
17 Ten Human-Driving Foibles: Deep Learning
18 Art of Defensive Driving is Key to Self-Driving Cars
19 Cyclops Approach to AI Self-Driving Cars is Myopic
20 Steering Wheel Gets Self-Driving Car Attention
21 Remote Piloting is a Self-Driving Car Crutch
22 Self-Driving Cars: Zero Fatalities, Zero Chance
23 Goldrush: Self-Driving Car Lawsuit Bonanza Ahead
24 Road Trip Trickery for Self-Driving Trucks and Cars
25 Ethically Ambiguous Self-Driving Car

This title is available via Amazon and other book sellers

Companion Book By This Author

Innovation and Thought Leadership on Self-Driving Driverless Cars

by Dr. Lance B. Eliot, MBA, PhD

Chapter Title

1 Sensor Fusion for Self-Driving Cars

2 Street Scene Free Space Detection Self-Driving Cars

3 Self-Awareness for Self-Driving Cars

4 Cartographic Trade-offs for Self-Driving Cars

5 Toll Road Traversal for Self-Driving Cars

6 Predictive Scenario Modeling for Self-Driving Cars

7 Selfishness for Self-Driving Cars

8 Leap Frog Driving for Self-Driving Cars

9 Proprioceptive IMU's for Self-Driving Cars

10 Robojacking of Self-Driving Cars

11 Self-Driving Car Moonshot and Mother of AI Projects

12 Marketing of Self-Driving Cars

13 Are Airplane Autopilots Same as Self-Driving Cars

14 Savvy Self-Driving Car Regulators: Marc Berman

15 Event Data Recorders (EDR) for Self-Driving Cars

16 Looking Behind You for Self-Driving Cars

17 In-Car Voice Commands NLP for Self-Driving Cars

18 When Self-Driving Cars Get Pulled Over by a Cop

19 Brainjacking Neuroprosthetus Self-Driving Cars

This title is available via Amazon and other book sellers

Companion Book By This Author

New Advances in AI Autonomous Driverless Cars Self-Driving Cars

by Dr. Lance B. Eliot, MBA, PhD

Chapter Title

1 Eliot Framework for AI Self-Driving Cars
2 Self-Driving Cars Learning from Self-Driving Cars
3 Imitation as Deep Learning for Self-Driving Cars
4 Assessing Federal Regulations for Self-Driving Cars
5 Bandwagon Effect for Self-Driving Cars
6 AI Backdoor Security Holes for Self-Driving Cars
7 Debiasing of AI for Self-Driving Cars
8 Algorithmic Transparency for Self-Driving Cars
9 Motorcycle Disentanglement for Self-Driving Cars
10 Graceful Degradation Handling of Self-Driving Cars
11 AI for Home Garage Parking of Self-Driving Cars
12 Motivational AI Irrationality for Self-Driving Cars
13 Curiosity as Cognition for Self-Driving Cars
14 Automotive Recalls of Self-Driving Cars
15 Internationalizing AI for Self-Driving Cars
16 Sleeping as AI Mechanism for Self-Driving Cars
17 Car Insurance Scams and Self-Driving Cars
18 U-Turn Traversal AI for Self-Driving Cars
19 Software Neglect for Self-Driving Cars

This title is available via Amazon and other book sellers

Companion Book By This Author

Introduction to Driverless Self-Driving Cars

by Dr. Lance B. Eliot, MBA, PhD

Chapter Title

1 Self-Driving Car Moonshot: Mother of All AI Projects
2 Grand Convergence Leads to Self-Driving Cars
3 Why They Should Be Called Self-Driving Cars
4 Richter Scale for Self-Driving Car Levels
5 LIDAR for Self-Driving Cars
6 Overall Framework for Self-Driving Cars
7 Sensor Fusion is Key for Self-Driving Cars
8 Humans Not Fast Enough for Self-Driving Cars
9 Solving Edge Problems of Self-Driving Cars
10 Graceful Degradation for Faltering Self-Driving Cars
11 Genetic Algorithms for Self-Driving Cars
12 Blockchain for Self-Driving Cars
13 Machine Learning and Data for Self-Driving Cars
14 Cyber-Hacking of Self-Driving Cars
15 Sensor Failures in Self-Driving Cars
16 When Accidents Happen to Self-Driving Cars
17 Backdoor Security Holes in Self-Driving Cars
18 Future Brainjacking for Self-Driving Cars
19 Internationalizing Self-Driving Cars
20 Are Airline Autopilots Same as Self-Driving Cars
21 Marketing of Self-Driving Cars
22 Fake News about Self-Driving Cars
23 Product Liability for Self-Driving Cars
24 Zero Fatalities Zero Chance for Self-Driving Cars
25 Road Trip Trickery for Self-Driving Cars
26 Ethical Issues of Self-Driving Cars
27 Ranking of Self-Driving Cars
28 Induced Demand Driven by Self-Driving Cars

This title is available via Amazon and other book sellers

Companion Book By This Author

Autonomous Vehicle Driverless Self-Driving Cars and Artificial Intelligence

by Dr. Lance B. Eliot, MBA, PhD

Chapter Title

1 Eliot Framework for AI Self-Driving Cars
2 Rocket Man Drivers and AI Self-Driving Cars
3 Occam's Razor Crucial for AI Self-Driving Cars
4 Simultaneous Local/Map (SLAM) for Self-Driving Cars
5 Swarm Intelligence for AI Self-Driving Cars
6 Biomimicry and Robomimicry for Self-Driving Cars
7 Deep Compression/Pruning for AI Self-Driving Cars
8 Extra-Scenery Perception for AI Self-Driving Cars
9 Invasive Curve and AI Self-Driving Cars
10 Normalization of Deviance and AI Self-Driving Cars
11 Groupthink Dilemma for AI Self-Driving Cars
12 Induced Demand Driven by AI Self-Driving Cars
13 Compressive Sensing for AI Self-Driving Cars
14 Neural Layer Explanations for AI Self-Driving Cars
15 Self-Adapting Resiliency for AI Self-Driving Cars
16 Prisoner's Dilemma and AI Self-Driving Cars
17 Turing Test and AI Self-Driving Cars
18 Support Vector Machines for AI Self-Driving Cars
19 "Expert Systems and AI Self-Driving Cars" by Michael Eliot

This title is available via Amazon and other book sellers

Companion Book By This Author

Transformative Artificial Intelligence Driverless Self-Driving Cars

by Dr. Lance B. Eliot, MBA, PhD

Chapter Title

1 Eliot Framework for AI Self-Driving Cars
2 Kinetosis Anti-Motion Sickness for Self-Driving Cars
3 Rain Driving for Self-Driving Cars
4 Edge Computing for Self-Driving Cars
5 Motorcycles as AI Self-Driving Vehicles
6 CAPTCHA Cyber-Hacking and Self-Driving Cars
7 Probabilistic Reasoning for Self-Driving Cars
8 Proving Grounds for Self-Driving Cars
9 Frankenstein and AI Self-Driving Cars
10 Omnipresence for Self-Driving Cars
11 Looking Behind You for Self-Driving Cars
12 Over-The-Air (OTA) Updating for Self-Driving Cars
13 Snow Driving for Self-Driving Cars
14 Human-Aided Training for Self-Driving Cars
15 Privacy for Self-Driving Cars
16 Transduction Vulnerabilities for Self-Driving Cars
17 Conversations Computing and Self-Driving Cars
18 Flying Debris and Self-Driving Cars
19 Citizen AI for Self-Driving Cars

This title is available via Amazon and other book sellers

Companion Book By This Author

Disruptive Artificial Intelligence and Driverless Self-Driving Cars

by Dr. Lance B. Eliot, MBA, PhD

Chapter Title

1 Eliot Framework for AI Self-Driving Cars

2 Maneuverability and Self-Driving Cars

3 Common Sense Reasoning and Self-Driving Cars

4 Cognition Timing and Self-Driving Cars

5 Speed Limits and Self-Driving Vehicles

6 Human Back-up Drivers and Self-Driving Cars

7 Forensic Analysis Uber and Self-Driving Cars

8 Power Consumption and Self-Driving Cars

9 Road Rage and Self-Driving Cars

10 Conspiracy Theories and Self-Driving Cars

11 Fear Landscape and Self-Driving Cars

12 Pre-Mortem and Self-Driving Cars

13 Kits and Self-Driving Cars

This title is available via Amazon and other book sellers

Companion Book By This Author

State-of-the-Art
AI Driverless Self-Driving Cars

by Dr. Lance B. Eliot, MBA, PhD

Chapter Title

1 Eliot Framework for AI Self-Driving Cars

2 Versioning and Self-Driving Cars

3 Towing and Self-Driving Cars

4 Driving Styles and Self-Driving Cars

5 Bicyclists and Self-Driving Vehicles

6 Back-up Cams and Self-Driving Cars

7 Traffic Mix and Self-Driving Cars

8 Hot-Car Deaths and Self-Driving Cars

9 Machine Learning Performance and Self-Driving Cars

10 Sensory Illusions and Self-Driving Cars

11 Federated Machine Learning and Self-Driving Cars

12 Irreproducibility and Self-Driving Cars

13 In-Car Deliveries and Self-Driving Cars

This title is available via Amazon and other book sellers

Companion Book By This Author

Top Trends in
AI Self-Driving Cars

by Dr. Lance B. Eliot, MBA, PhD

Chapter Title

1 Eliot Framework for AI Self-Driving Cars

2 Responsibility and Self-Driving Cars

3 Changing Lanes and Self-Driving Cars

4 Procrastination and Self-Driving Cars

5 NTSB Report and Tesla Car Crash

6 Start Over AI and Self-Driving Cars

7 Freezing Robot Problem and Self-Driving Cars

8 Canarying and Self-Driving Cars

9 Nighttime Driving and Self-Driving Cars

10 Zombie-Cars Taxes and Self-Driving Cars

11 Traffic Lights and Self-Driving Cars

12 Reverse Engineering and Self-Driving Cars

13 Singularity AI and Self-Driving Cars

This title is available via Amazon and other book sellers

Companion Book By This Author

AI Innovations and Self-Driving Cars

by Dr. Lance B. Eliot, MBA, PhD

Chapter Title

1 Eliot Framework for AI Self-Driving Cars

2 API's and Self-Driving Cars

3 Egocentric Designs and Self-Driving Cars

4 Family Road Trip and Self-Driving Cars

5 AI Developer Burnout and Tesla Car Crash

6 Stealing Secrets About Self-Driving Cars

7 Affordability and Self-Driving Cars

8 Crossing the Rubicon and Self-Driving Cars

9 Addicted to Self-Driving Cars

10 Ultrasonic Harm and Self-Driving Cars

11 Accidents Contagion and Self-Driving Cars

12 Non-Stop 24x7 and Self-Driving Cars

13 Human Life Spans and Self-Driving Cars

This title is available via Amazon and other book sellers

Companion Book By This Author

Crucial Advances for
AI Self-Driving Cars

by Dr. Lance B. Eliot, MBA, PhD

Chapter Title

1 Eliot Framework for AI Self-Driving Cars

2 Ensemble Learning and AI Self-Driving Cars

3 Ghost in AI Self-Driving Cars

4 Public Shaming of AI Self-Driving

5 Internet of Things (IoT) and AI Self-Driving Cars

6 Personal Rapid Transit (RPT) and Self-Driving Cars

7 Eventual Consistency and AI Self-Driving Cars

8 Mass Transit Future and AI Self-Driving Cars

9 Coopetition and AI Self-Driving Cars

10 Electric Vehicles (EVs) and AI Self-Driving Cars

11 Dangers of In-Motion AI Self-Driving Cars

12 Sports Cars and AI Self-Driving Cars

13 Game Theory and AI Self-Driving Cars

This title is available via Amazon and other book sellers

Companion Book By This Author

Sociotechnical Insights and AI Driverless Cars

by Dr. Lance B. Eliot, MBA, PhD

Chapter Title

1 Eliot Framework for AI Self-Driving Cars
2 Start-ups and AI Self-Driving Cars
3 Code Obfuscation and AI Self-Driving Cars
4 Hyperlanes and AI Self-Driving Cars
5 Passenger Panic Inside an AI Self-Driving Car
6 Tech Stockholm Syndrome and Self-Driving Cars
7 Paralysis and AI Self-Driving Cars
8 Ugly Zones and AI Self-Driving Cars
9 Ridesharing and AI Self-Driving Cars
10 Multi-Party Privacy and AI Self-Driving Cars
11 Chaff Bugs and AI Self-Driving Cars
12 Social Reciprocity and AI Self-Driving Cars
13 Pet Mode and AI Self-Driving Cars

This title is available via Amazon and other book sellers

Companion Book By This Author

Pioneering Advances for AI Driverless Cars

by Dr. Lance B. Eliot, MBA, PhD

Chapter Title

1 Eliot Framework for AI Self-Driving Cars

2 Boxes on Wheels and AI Self-Driving Cars

3 Clogs and AI Self-Driving Cars

4 Kids Communicating with AI Self-Driving Cars

5 Incident Awareness and AI Self-Driving Car

6 Emotion Recognition and Self-Driving Cars

7 Rear-End Collisions and AI Self-Driving Cars

8 Autonomous Nervous System and AI Self-Driving Cars

9 Height Warnings and AI Self-Driving Cars

10 Future Jobs and AI Self-Driving Cars

11 Car Wash and AI Self-Driving Cars

12 5G and AI Self-Driving Cars

13 Gen Z and AI Self-Driving Cars

This title is available via Amazon and other book sellers

Companion Book By This Author

Leading Edge Trends for AI Driverless Cars

by Dr. Lance B. Eliot, MBA, PhD

Chapter Title

1 Eliot Framework for AI Self-Driving Cars

2 Pranking and AI Self-Driving Cars

3 Drive-Thrus and AI Self-Driving Cars

4 Overworking on AI Self-Driving Cars

5 Sleeping Barber Problem and AI Self-Driving Cars

6 System Load Balancing and AI Self-Driving Cars

7 Virtual Spike Strips and AI Self-Driving Cars

8 Razzle Dazzle Camouflage and AI Self-Driving Cars

9 Rewilding of AI Self-Driving Cars

10 Brute Force Algorithms and AI Self-Driving Cars

11 Idle Moments and AI Self-Driving Cars

12 Hurricanes and AI Self-Driving Cars

13 Object Visual Transplants and AI Self-Driving Cars

This title is available via Amazon and other book sellers

Companion Book By This Author

The Cutting Edge of AI Autonomous Cars

by Dr. Lance B. Eliot, MBA, PhD

Chapter Title

1 Eliot Framework for AI Self-Driving Cars

2 Driving Controls and AI Self-Driving Cars

3 Bug Bounty and AI Self-Driving Cars

4 Lane Splitting and AI Self-Driving Cars

5 Drunk Drivers versus AI Self-Driving Cars

6 Internal Naysayers and AI Self-Driving Cars

7 Debugging and AI Self-Driving Cars

8 Ethics Review Boards and AI Self-Driving Cars

9 Road Diets and AI Self-Driving Cars

10 Wrong Way Driving and AI Self-Driving Cars

11 World Safety Summit and AI Self-Driving Cars

This title is available via Amazon and other book sellers

Companion Book By This Author

The Next Wave of AI Self-Driving Cars

by Dr. Lance B. Eliot, MBA, PhD

Chapter Title

1 Eliot Framework for AI Self-Driving Cars

2 Productivity and AI Self-Driving Cars

3 Blind Pedestrians and AI Self-Driving Cars

4 Fail-Safe AI and AI Self-Driving Cars

5 Anomaly Detection and AI Self-Driving Cars

6 Running Out of Gas and AI Self-Driving Cars

7 Deep Personalization and AI Self-Driving Cars

8 Reframing the Levels of AI Self-Driving Cars

9 Cryptojacking and AI Self-Driving Cars

Companion Book By This Author

Revolutionary Innovations of AI Self-Driving Cars

by Dr. Lance B. Eliot, MBA, PhD

Chapter Title

1 Eliot Framework for AI Self-Driving Cars

2 Exascale Supercomputer and AI Self-Driving Cars

3 Superhuman AI and AI Self-Driving Cars

4 Olfactory e-Nose Sensors and AI Self-Driving Cars

5 Perpetual Computing and AI Self-Driving Cars

6 Byzantine Generals Problem and AI Self-Driving Cars

7 Driver Traffic Guardians and AI Self-Driving Cars

8 Anti-Gridlock Laws and AI Self-Driving Cars

9 Arguing Machines and AI Self-Driving Cars

This title is available via Amazon and other book sellers

Companion Book By This Author

AI Self-Driving Cars
Breakthroughs

by Dr. Lance B. Eliot, MBA, PhD

Chapter Title

1 Eliot Framework for AI Self-Driving Cars

2 Off-Roading and AI Self-Driving Cars

3 Paralleling Vehicles and AI Self-Driving Cars

4 Dementia Drivers and AI Self-Driving Cars

5 Augmented Realty (AR) and AI Self-Driving Cars

6 Sleeping Inside an AI Self-Driving Car

7 Prevalence Detection and AI Self-Driving Cars

8 Super-Intelligent AI and AI Self-Driving Cars

9 Car Caravans and AI Self-Driving Cars

This title is available via Amazon and other book sellers

Companion Book By This Author

***Trailblazing Trends for* AI Self-Driving Cars**

by Dr. Lance B. Eliot, MBA, PhD

Chapter Title

1 Eliot Framework for AI Self-Driving Cars

2 Strategic AI Metaphors and AI Self-Driving Cars

3 Emergency-Only AI and AI Self-Driving Cars

4 Animal Drawn Vehicles and AI Self-Driving Cars

5 Chess Play and AI Self-Driving Cars

6 Cobots Exoskeletons and AI Self-Driving Car

7 Economic Commodity and AI Self-Driving Cars

8 Road Racing and AI Self-Driving Cars

This title is available via Amazon and other book sellers

Companion Book By This Author

Ingenious Strides for
AI Driverless Cars

by Dr. Lance B. Eliot, MBA, PhD

Chapter Title

1 Eliot Framework for AI Self-Driving Cars

2 Plasticity and AI Self-Driving Cars

3 NIMBY vs. YIMBY and AI Self-Driving Cars

4 Top Trends for 2019 and AI Self-Driving Cars

5 Rural Areas and AI Self-Driving Cars

6 Self-Imposed Constraints and AI Self-Driving Car

7 Alien Limb Syndrome and AI Self-Driving Cars

8 Jaywalking and AI Self-Driving Cars

This title is available via Amazon and other book sellers

Companion Book By This Author

AI Self-Driving Cars Inventiveness

by Dr. Lance B. Eliot, MBA, PhD

Chapter Title

1 Eliot Framework for AI Self-Driving Cars

2 Crumbling Infrastructure and AI Self-Driving Cars

3 e-Billboarding and AI Self-Driving Cars

4 Kinship and AI Self-Driving Cars

5 Machine-Child Learning and AI Self-Driving Cars

6 Baby-on-Board and AI Self-Driving Car

7 Cop Car Chases and AI Self-Driving Cars

8 One-Shot Learning and AI Self-Driving Cars

This title is available via Amazon and other book sellers

Companion Book By This Author

Visionary Secrets of AI Driverless Cars

by Dr. Lance B. Eliot, MBA, PhD

Chapter Title

1 Eliot Framework for AI Self-Driving Cars
2 Seat Belts and AI Self-Driving Cars
3 Tiny EV's and AI Self-Driving Cars
4 Empathetic Computing and AI Self-Driving Cars
5 Ethics Global Variations and AI Self-Driving Cars
6 Computational Periscopy and AI Self-Driving Car
7 Superior Cognition and AI Self-Driving Cars
8 Amalgamating ODD's and AI Self-Driving Cars

This title is available via Amazon and other book sellers

Companion Book By This Author

Spearheading
AI Self-Driving Cars

by Dr. Lance B. Eliot, MBA, PhD

Chapter Title

1 Eliot Framework for AI Self-Driving Cars

2 Artificial Pain and AI Self-Driving Cars

3 Stop-and-Frisks and AI Self-Driving Cars

4 Cars Careening and AI Self-Driving Cars

5 Sounding Out Car Noises and AI Self-Driving Cars

6 No Speed Limit Autobahn and AI Self-Driving Car

7 Noble Cause Corruption and AI Self-Driving Cars

8 AI Rockstars and AI Self-Driving Cars

This title is available via Amazon and other book sellers

Companion Book By This Author

Spurring
AI Self-Driving Cars

by Dr. Lance B. Eliot, MBA, PhD

Chapter Title

1 Eliot Framework for AI Self-Driving Cars

2 Triune Brain Theory and AI Self-Driving Cars

3 Car Parts Thefts and AI Self-Driving Cars

4 Goto Fail Bug and AI Self-Driving Cars

5 Scrabble Understanding and AI Self-Driving Cars

6 Cognition Disorders and AI Self-Driving Car

7 Noise Pollution Abatement AI Self-Driving Cars

This title is available via Amazon and other book sellers

Companion Book By This Author

Avant-Garde
AI Driverless Cars

by Dr. Lance B. Eliot, MBA, PhD

Chapter Title

1 Eliot Framework for AI Self-Driving Cars

2 Linear Non-Threshold and AI Self-Driving Cars

3 Prediction Equation and AI Self-Driving Cars

4 Modular Autonomous Systems and AI Self-Driving Cars

5 Driver's Licensing and AI Self-Driving Cars

6 Offshoots and Spinoffs and AI Self-Driving Car

7 Depersonalization and AI Self-Driving Cars

This title is available via Amazon and other book sellers

Companion Book By This Author

AI Self-Driving Cars Evolvement

by Dr. Lance B. Eliot, MBA, PhD

Chapter Title

1 Eliot Framework for AI Self-Driving Cars

2 Chief Safety Officers and AI Self-Driving Cars

3 Bounded Volumes and AI Self-Driving Cars

4 Micro-Movements Behaviors and AI Self-Driving Cars

5 Boeing 737 Aspects and AI Self-Driving Cars

6 Car Controls Commands and AI Self-Driving Car

7 Multi-Sensor Data Fusion and AI Self-Driving Cars

This title is available via Amazon and other book sellers

Companion Book By This Author

AI Driverless Cars Chrysalis

by Dr. Lance B. Eliot, MBA, PhD

Chapter Title

1 Eliot Framework for AI Self-Driving Cars
2 Object Poses and AI Self-Driving Cars
3 Human In-The-Loop and AI Self-Driving Cars
4 Genius Shortage and AI Self-Driving Cars
5 Salvage Yards and AI Self-Driving Cars
6 Precision Scheduling and AI Self-Driving Car
7 Human Driving Extinction and AI Self-Driving Cars

This title is available via Amazon and other book sellers

Companion Book By This Author

Boosting
AI Autonomous Cars

by Dr. Lance B. Eliot, MBA, PhD

Chapter Title

1 Eliot Framework for AI Self-Driving Cars

2 Zero Knowledge Proofs and AI Self-Driving Cars

3 Active Shooter Response and AI Self-Driving Cars

4 Free Will and AI Self-Driving Cars

5 No Picture Yet of AI Self-Driving Cars

6 Boeing 737 Lessons and AI Self-Driving Cars

7 Preview Tesla FSD and AI Self-Driving Cars

8 LIDAR Industry and AI Self-Driving Cars

9 Uber IPO and AI Self-Driving Cars

10 Suing Automakers of AI Self-Driving Cars

11 Tesla Overarching FSD and AI Self-Driving Cars

12 Auto Repair Market and AI Self-Driving Cars

This title is available via Amazon and other book sellers

Companion Book By This Author

AI Self-Driving Cars
Trendsetting

by Dr. Lance B. Eliot, MBA, PhD

Chapter Title

1 Eliot Framework for AI Self-Driving Cars
2 OTA Myths and AI Self-Driving Cars
3 Surveys and AI Self-Driving Cars
4 Tech Spies and AI Self-Driving Cars
5 Anxieties and AI Self-Driving Cars
6 Achilles Heel and AI Self-Driving Cars
7 Kids Alone and AI Self-Driving Cars
8 Infrastructure and AI Self-Driving Cars
9 Distracted Driving and AI Self-Driving Cars
10 Human Drivers and AI Self-Driving Cars
11 Anti-LIDAR Stance and AI Self-Driving Cars
12 Autopilot Team and AI Self-Driving Cars
13 Rigged Videos and AI Self-Driving Cars
14 Stalled Cars and AI Self-Driving Cars
15 Princeton Summit and AI Self-Driving Cars
16 Brittleness and AI Self-Driving Cars
17 Mergers and AI Self-Driving Cars

This title is available via Amazon and other book sellers

Companion Book By This Author

AI Autonomous Cars Forefront

by Dr. Lance B. Eliot, MBA, PhD

Chapter Title

1 Eliot Framework for AI Self-Driving Cars
2 Essential Stats and AI Self-Driving Cars
3 Stats Fallacies and AI Self-Driving Cars
4 Driver Bullies and AI Self-Driving Cars
5 Sunday Drives and AI Self-Driving Cars
6 Face Recog Bans and AI Self-Driving Cars
7 States On-The-Hook and AI Self-Driving Cars
8 Sensors Profiting and AI Self-Driving Cars
9 Unruly Riders and AI Self-Driving Cars
10 Father's Day and AI Self-Driving Cars
11 Summons Feature and AI Self-Driving Cars
12 Libra Cryptocurrency and AI Self-Driving Cars
13 Systems Naming and AI Self-Driving Cars
14 Mid-Traffic Rendezvous and AI Self-Driving Cars
15 Pairing Drones and AI Self-Driving Cars
16 Lost Wallet Study and AI Self-Driving Cars

This title is available via Amazon and other book sellers

ABOUT THE AUTHOR

Dr. Lance B. Eliot, MBA, PhD is the CEO of Techbruim, Inc. and Executive Director of the Cybernetic AI Self-Driving Car Institute, and has over twenty years of industry experience including serving as a corporate officer in a billion dollar firm and was a partner in a major executive services firm. He is also a serial entrepreneur having founded, ran, and sold several high-tech related businesses. He previously hosted the popular radio show *Technotrends* that was also available on American Airlines flights via their in-flight audio program. Author or co-author of a dozen books and over 400 articles, he has made appearances on CNN, and has been a frequent speaker at industry conferences.

A former professor at the University of Southern California (USC), he founded and led an innovative research lab on Artificial Intelligence in Business. Known as the "AI Insider" his writings on AI advances and trends has been widely read and cited. He also previously served on the faculty of the University of California Los Angeles (UCLA), and was a visiting professor at other major universities. He was elected to the International Board of the Society for Information Management (SIM), a prestigious association of over 3,000 high-tech executives worldwide.

He has performed extensive community service, including serving as Senior Science Adviser to the Vice Chair of the Congressional Committee on Science & Technology. He has served on the Board of the OC Science & Engineering Fair (OCSEF), where he is also has been a Grand Sweepstakes judge, and likewise served as a judge for the Intel International SEF (ISEF). He served as the Vice Chair of the Association for Computing Machinery (ACM) Chapter, a prestigious association of computer scientists. Dr. Eliot has been a shark tank judge for the USC Mark Stevens Center for Innovation on start-up pitch competitions, and served as a mentor for several incubators and accelerators in Silicon Valley and Silicon Beach. He served on several Boards and Committees at USC, including having served on the Marshall Alumni Association (MAA) Board in Southern California.

Dr. Eliot holds a PhD from USC, MBA, and Bachelor's in Computer Science, and earned the CDP, CCP, CSP, CDE, and CISA certifications. Born and raised in Southern California, and having traveled and lived internationally, he enjoys scuba diving, surfing, and sailing.

ADDENDUM

AI Autonomous Cars Forefront

Practical Advances in Artificial Intelligence (AI) and Machine Learning

By

Dr. Lance B. Eliot, MBA, PhD

For supplemental materials of this book, visit:

www.ai-selfdriving-cars.guru

For special orders of this book, contact:

LBE Press Publishing

Email: LBE.Press.Publishing@gmail.com

www.ingramcontent.com/pod-product-compliance
Lightning Source LLC
Chambersburg PA
CBHW051047050326
40690CB00006B/629
9781733249829